1945-1995

50 Years of Publishing

THE CHILDREN'S
JEWISH HOLIDAY KITCHEN

BOOKS BY JOAN NATHAN

THE CHILDREN'S JEWISH HOLIDAY KITCHEN

70 ways to have fun with your kids
and make your family's celebrations special

JOAN NATHAN

ILLUSTRATED BY BROOKE SCUDDER

Schocken Books   New York

Grateful acknowledgment is made to *Kashrus* magazine for the collage on p. xii,
which includes a sampling of the over 200 symbols used by kosher certifying agencies.
The collage was produced by *Kashrus* magazine, P.O. Box 204, Brooklyn, NY 11204,
which monitors all kosher certifications. Reprinted by permission.

Library of Congress Cataloging-in-Publication Data
Nathan, Joan.
The children's Jewish holiday kitchen: 70 ways to have fun with your kids
and make your family's celebrations special / Joan Nathan.
p.   cm.
Includes index.
ISBN 0-8052-4130-2
1. Cookery, Jewish—Juvenile literature.   2. Holiday cookery—
Juvenile literature.   [1. Cookery, Jewish.]   I. Title.
TX724.N367   1995
641.5′676—dc20   95-5981
AC

BOOK DESIGN BY FEARN CUTLER

Manufactured in the United States of America
2 4 6 8 9 7 5 3

To Daniela, Merissa, and David

ACKNOWLEDGMENTS

Writing a cookbook always involves the help of many people. I would like to thank the following friends and family for expert advice, ideas, and recipes: Susan Barocas, Beverly I. Colman, Mickey Feinberg, Paula Gerson, Ellen Gold, Mary Lynn Goldstein, Anne Kampelman, Reba Leand, the late Rabbi Eugene Lipman, Charlotte Muchnick, Ellen Neschis, Dorothy Regensteiner, Cantor Arnold Saltzman, Marian Sofaer, Mark Talisman, Elizabeth Wallace, and Barbara Winnik. I would also like to thank Adas Israel's Gan Ha-Yeled and Jewish Primary Day School for introducing my children to so many Jewish customs.

CONTENTS

PREFACE

Since the first edition of this book was published in 1987, I have watched my children grow. My eldest daughter, Daniela, is off to college next year, while Merissa just celebrated her Bat Mitzvah. Their brother, David, an infant in 1987, is now an aspiring young actor. Amidst the ever-changing kaleidoscope of their lives at home and at school, the table has been a constant in binding us together as a family.

We continue to try to make time each evening for a meal together, a refreshing pause when we can catch up with each of our children, and they with us! And how relaxing it is to talk while snipping beans or shelling peas. This book is a testimony to that time together. It includes twenty new recipes which we as a family use and have developed. Also over the years, as we have traveled, we have learned many things and acquired new tastes. Many of these are shared in this new edition, like snacking on pomegranates and using prepared puff pastry to make knishes.

As our children have grown they have become less interested in meat, and more in vegetarian meals with low fat content. And they have definite ideas of what they like. As David told me when I was preparing this new edition of the book, "Mom, kids like plain lasagna, no lumps in their food. They like smooth tomato sauce!" I could have added for him that they also like every dessert with chocolate chips.

Through the years as I travel the country speaking about Jewish food, I have been gratified to discover how many children have learned to cook from these recipes. Now my daughters and their friends can use this book on their own. Luckily for me, David still needs my help!

Shabbat and the Jewish holidays have always remained special times for us. My husband, Allan, and I, my children, family, and friends have created so many wonderful memories, not just of the holiday observances themselves, but of the preparations as well. Because of the symbolic dishes associated with Judaism, food is a perfect vehicle to introduce children to the many aspects of their religion. They will feel good about helping to prepare the holiday and Sabbath meals. Just remember: a meal doesn't have to be heavy to be Jewish!

The aims of this book are the same as they were when it was first published: simply, to have fun making Jewish holiday recipes that the whole family can enjoy; to teach children some of the basics of cooking and baking; and, in the process, to explore and explain the meaning and history behind Jewish food. The premise is that cooking will be a cooperative effort between adults and children.

The Children's Jewish Holiday Kitchen is divided into ten holidays, with menus and recipes for each. As I have discovered from going through these celebrations with my children, meaning and memories are greatly enhanced when we all participate together in the preparations.

All of the recipes specify the ingredients, equipment, and steps suitable for children to do by themselves or with adults or older children. The adult will assign tasks to match the skill of the cooks. Starred (*) menu items are dishes for which recipes are given. Cooking skills such as separating eggs, using knives, rolling out piecrust, blanching almonds, and proofing yeast are explained in the course of the recipes. Learning these basic skills will serve your children well throughout all their days in the kitchen.

The foods are those that children and adults alike will enjoy, and use only wholesome ingredients. We have used real Jewish holiday recipes, some of which have been simplified for children but still satisfy adult taste buds. We have shared the culinary traditions we especially like in our family, omitting those that are not child-centered.

The recipes represent a sampling from Israel and many of the countries in the Jewish Diaspora. Many include stories, some about the way grandparents and other ancestors, going back through Europe and the Orient to ancient Palestine, may have served the food on their own tables. Still others, like the cupcake menorah for Hanukkah or the matzah pizza, are American.

In addition to the recipes themselves, *The Children's Jewish Holiday Kitchen* shows how a family can celebrate the holidays and enjoy craft activities such as making hallah covers and candlesticks, and includes hints for introducing children to the Torah portion of the week. Tips for making hallahs for large or small families are also given.

One last word to the wise parent or older child should be sufficient: before you begin cooking, fill your sink with warm, sudsy water and bright-colored sponges. Let your children know early on that cleaning up as they go along is part of the activity.

Above all, as we worked on this expanded book and the recipes that are part of our weekly ritual, we enjoyed learning even more about the blessings and traditions, cooking with our friends and eating our creations during and after the cooking process was finished. When I first wrote this book my children treated cookie dough like Play-Doh. Now, I am happy to say, they are great start-from-scratch cooks. For me, personally, one of the benefits of cooking with my own children is that it gives us a chance to talk and to relax together. I hope you will have as much pleasure cooking from this book with your family as I have with my own.

KASHRUT
HOW DO WE KNOW WHAT IS KOSHER?

For three thousand years Jews have adhered to dietary laws. These laws were written in the Bible.

"Whatsoever parteth the hoof, and is wholly cloven-footed, and cheweth the cud . . . that may ye eat" (Leviticus 11:3). With the help of illustrated books or magazines, let the children discover which meats are permissible for Jews to eat, and why. Beef, veal, lamb, and mutton are a few; any part of a pig is forbidden. But what about a lion? A gerbil? A unicorn? A dinosaur? This exercise can be fun, as well as instructive.

As specific as the Bible is about red-meat animals, it is equally vague about fowl. Twenty-four kinds of birds are specifically prohibited in Leviticus 11:13–19; these are mainly birds of prey, such as the eagle, vulture, raven, owl, and hawk. Some permissible poultry that we eat in this country are turkey, goose, duck, and that Friday-night wonder, chicken.

"These may ye eat of all that are in the waters: whatsoever hath fins and scales in the waters, in the seas, and in the rivers, them may ye eat" (Leviticus 11:9). A clean fish must have both fins and scales, and the scales must be detachable from the skin. Bluefish, salmon, cod, scrod, flounder, whitefish, carp, pike, and sole are all allowed. Shellfish, such as shrimp, lobster, clams, and oysters, lack fins and scales and are scavengers. They are not kosher (fit to eat). But seahorses? Creatures in Jules Verne's books? Take a look!

Many cities have a Kashrut Board with a telephone service you can call with any questions that come up.

Before any meat is eaten, the animal must be slaughtered in a kosher manner. A limb torn or cut from a living animal is forbidden. An animal that is not slaughtered, but that dies of itself, is also prohibited. Only select animals, thoroughly tested, are used. What is particularly important to Jews is the fact that for thousands of years so many of them have adhered to this prohibition.

Kashrut

Another Jewish distinction is the way in which animals are slaughtered. The rules for slaughtering spring from ethical principles and are also designed to reject the sacrificial practices of paganism. "Thou shalt kill thy herd and thy flock, which the Lord hath given thee, as I have commanded thee, and thou shalt eat within thy gates, after all the desire of the soul" (Deuteronomy 12:21). All meat animals and birds require *shehitah*, the ritual slaughtering with a very clean, sharp knife. The *shohet* (slaughterer) follows a tradition dating back three thousand years to the meat sacrificed at the Temple in Jerusalem when he says, "Blessed art Thou, O Lord our God, King of the universe, who hast commanded us in the ritual of slaughtering."

The Bible says that one must not eat blood. "Therefore I said unto the children of Israel: No soul of you shall eat blood. . . . Ye shall eat the blood of no manner of flesh. . . . whosoever eateth it shall be cut off" (Leviticus 17:12, 14). After all the blood is removed by soaking in cold water for half an hour, the meat is salted for one hour with coarse kosher rather than fine-grained salt (which would dissolve instead of drawing out the blood). Then the salt is shaken off and the meat washed three times so that no blood remains.

Another dietary law prohibits cooking or eating meat and milk together: "Thou shalt not seethe a kid in its mother's milk" (Deuteronomy 14:20). The purpose of this law was to prevent the ancient Hebrews from following pagan customs of animal sacrifice. It was also a way of helping digestion. Two separate sets of utensils must be provided for the preparation, serving, and storing of milk and meat dishes. The utensils must be washed separately. Traditional Jews may have two sinks and two sets of sponges, mixing bowls, and dishes, or two sets of blades and bowls for mixers and food processors. Between a milk and a meat meal, one must merely rinse out the mouth or eat a morsel of bread. For this, there is no waiting requirement. Between a meat and a milk meal, however, where digestion is more difficult, Jews wait anywhere from one to six hours.

Neutral or *pareve* foods, such as fish, eggs, and vegetables, may be used with either milk or meat. Some Jews will not eat *pareve* foods outside the home for fear that they may have been cooked in a forbidden fat (lard, or butter during a meat meal).

Many packaged foods are marked with symbols such as Ⓤ or Ⓚ to indicate that a Jewish organization has approved them as kosher. There are a number of different symbols in various parts of the country.

Even if you are not kosher, your children should be made aware of the dietary laws. Visit a kosher butcher and watch the koshering of meat. Go to buy the hallah at a Jewish bakery and have someone explain the difference between *pareve* and *milchig* (milk) bakery products. Take a field trip to your local grocery store and have a scavenger hunt, letting the children identify products to see which soups, cereals, etc., are marked with the Ⓤ or Ⓚ and/or the word *pareve* on the packages. They (and you) will be surprised at how universal the markings have become.

SABBATH

WINTER FRIDAY NIGHT MENU

Grape Juice*
Hallah*
Matzah Ball Soup*
Strips of Green Peppers, Cucumbers, and Carrots
Friday Night Pot Roast*
Fruit Kugel*
Daniela's Brownies*

SUMMER FRIDAY NIGHT MENU

Kids' Quicky Knishes*
Tree of Life Salad with Hummus*
Turkey Tenders*
Mixed Berries

WINTER SATURDAY LUNCH MENU

Hallah*
Vegetarian Chopped Liver*
Children's Cholent*
Jaffa Orange Sorbet*

SUMMER SATURDAY LUNCH MENU

Hallah*
Cream Cheese or Spinach Burekas*
Cucumber-Yoghurt Salad*
Mandelbrot*

SABBATH

In America today, the way each family spends the Sabbath is highly personal. In our family, we desperately need to slow down and spend time together. When our children were younger, sitting still in the synagogue was difficult for them. Whereas my husband, Allan, would occasionally take the older children, I found it extremely difficult with an infant, so I preferred taking long walks as a family or hanging around the house. Now we are at the Bar and Bat Mitzvah stage and find special meaning in going to synagogue as a family.

Our favorite time of the week is Friday night, when everything relaxes. I always remember when I lived in Jerusalem and there was that frantic rush to prepare for the Sabbath. Mothers breathed a sigh of relief when all the preparations were completed, because they could relax.

Now we rarely go out on Friday night and often invite other families to dine with us. When the children were small, they drew a decorated menu before each Sabbath, with stars to show which dishes they had cooked themselves (this also alerted adults to the tenor of the meal and let them know that extravagant compliments would not be out of place!).

We set a pretty table, more often than not with a white tablecloth, fresh flowers, white candles, our best china, and a hallah which we bake together. The hallah is placed on a silver platter my father brought to this country when he emigrated from Germany. The hallah cover alternates between one made by Merissa in school and one stitched by a grandmother. Everybody has his own kiddush cup, some filled with white or red wine, others with apple or grape juice.

Standing at the table, Daniela, Merissa, and I cover our eyes. Then, together we say the blessings over the candles:

Baruch atah Adonai Eloheinu melech ha-olam,
asher kidshanu b'mitzvotav ve-tzivanu l'hadlik
ner shel Shabbat.

Blessed art Thou, O Lord our God, King of the universe,
who hast sanctified us by Thy commandments,
and commanded us to kindle the Sabbath lights.

Allan says the blessings over the wine and the bread in our family, but in many of our friends' families everyone says the blessings together:

Baruch atah Adonai Eloheinu melech ha-olam,
borei p'ri ha-gafen.
Blessed art Thou, O Lord our God,
King of the universe, who createst the fruit of the vine.

We all sip the wine. Then Allan says the blessing over the hallah:

Baruch atah Adonai Eloheinu melech ha-olam,
ha-motzi lechem min ha-aretz.
Blessed art Thou, O Lord our God, King of the universe,
who bringest forth bread from the earth.

Then one of the children breaks off pieces of bread to pass to everyone who is at the table. They find it more fun to rip apart the hallah on Friday night than to cut it with a knife. For some people, this custom is also symbolic of the special peacefulness of the Sabbath.

Then Allan spreads his hands over the heads of the girls and blesses them:

Y'simech Elohim k'Sarah, Rivka, Rahel v'Leah.
May God bless you like Sarah, Rebecca, Rachel, and Leah.

For our son, David, he says,

Y'simecha Elohim k'Ephraim v'hi-Menasheh.
May God bless you like Ephraim and Menasheh.

Then we kiss each of our children and say,

Shabbat shalom.

Allan sometimes tells a story from the week's Torah portion, gearing his short talk to the age of our children, sometimes linking what he has to say to the news of the week. Often he will test them by asking questions from the week before. The *Jerusalem Post* and the local Jewish newspaper include commentaries on the portion of the week. Good books to buy are Nehama Leibowitz's six-book series *Studies in the Torah* (Jerusalem, 1980) and *The Way of the Torah* by David Epstein (New York, 1986). Occasionally we sing Hebrew and Yiddish songs. When they have finished the main course, our children still leave the room to prepare a skit, often from the Bible, which they perform before dessert.

SABBATH COOKING CRAFTS

In order to make your children feel part of the Sabbath ritual or that of any holiday, let them make their own hallah board, hallah cover, kiddush cup, and whatever else is called for.

Hallah board: Use any old board that seems the shape you would like for a hallah board. Sand the wood. Let the children paint it or even make handprints in finger paint and shellac it.

Hallah cover: Use a piece of cotton or other non–water-repellent fabric. Place water in jars with vegetable skins for color: grapes for purple, onion skins for brown, beets for red, parsley for green. Zap them in the microwave or boil until you get the color you wish. The children can then use a paintbrush or medicine droppers to color the cover. This is an especially nice task at Rosh Hashanah or Sukkot, with the different fruits and vegetables of the harvest used as the paints. Rinse the cover in vinegar, which will set the color.

Shabbat place mats: Let the children paint or color cardboard or durable construction paper. Then cover with clear contact paper or even plastic wrap. Tape the place mat down.

Kiddush cups: Have the children decorate plastic cups with permanent marking pens and write the name of each family member and guest on them. They can then be used as place cards as well.

Candlestick holders: Have the children make the holders out of home-made clay. Mix together 4 cups flour, 1 cup salt, and about 1½ cups water to make a stiff dough. Divide the dough into balls the size of Ping-Pong balls. The children can mold them as they wish. Then, while the dough is still soft, they insert the candle they will use to make a hole.

GRAPE JUICE

In India, the eldest daughter's role is to make grape juice fresh each Thursday for the Sabbath meal. When dark grapes are not available, she uses dried black raisins that are soaked in water, then boiled. In India, hallah is more like our matzah, and the Sabbath meal more often than not includes a spicy lamb or chicken curry.

Wherever you live, the following prayer is said over the wine every Friday night. To children in Israel at the time of the Bible, this meant grape juice—not apple or other fruit juices.

Baruch atah Adonai Eloheinu melech ha-olam,
borei p'ri ha-gafen.
Blessed art Thou, O Lord our God, King of the universe,
who createst the fruit of the vine.

INGREDIENTS

4 cups Concord, Thompson,
   or Ribier grapes
⅓ cup water
1 cup sugar, or to taste

EQUIPMENT

Measuring cups
2 large pots, 1 with a lid
Large spoon for each child
Colander
Serving pitcher

MAKES
ABOUT
6 CUPS

Child: Wash the grapes and remove the stems. Place the grapes and the water in a large pot. Cover and cook over low heat, stirring occasionally, until the fruit is softened, about 20 minutes.

Adult: When the fruit is squeezable, place it in a large colander over an empty pot.

Child: Press the fruit with a spoon to squeeze the juice out. To every 6 cups grape juice, add 1 cup sugar, or make it as sweet as you like. Stir until the sugar dissolves and the juice cools. Serve cold in a pretty pitcher.

HALLAH

My husband's mother, who came to this country from a small town in Poland, told Daniela and Merissa the story of how her mother baked the hallah each Friday. Before making the braided twists of bread, she would break off a morsel of dough and throw it into the wood-burning stove as a reminder of the burnt offering made at the Temple in Jerusalem long ago. During the week, the family bought rye bread and white rolls for breakfast at a local bakery. Friday was reserved for the sweet hallah.

Before the hallah is eaten, a prayer is always recited over it. In the Friday night blessing ritual, this bread symbolizes all food that comes from the earth.

Baruch atah Adonai Eloheinu melech ha-olam,
ha-motzi lehem min ha-aretz.
Blessed art Thou, O Lord our God, King of the universe,
who bringest forth bread from the earth.

Hallah baking hints: The following recipe makes three normal-size breads. If your family is small and you don't want to use the leftovers for breakfast, experiment with forming the bread into four or even five loaves, freezing them for a month of Sabbaths. We make Thursday our hallah day. I prepare the dough in the morning with the girls, then let it rise (first in the kitchen and then in the refrigerator). Just before the children come home from school, I remove it from the refrigerator. They and their friends literally punch the dough down and braid the loaves themselves—after all, forming the twists is what they like to do best.

We usually make two hallah twists and freeze one if there are no guests. We roll the last third of the dough into a rectangle, sprinkling about ½ cup sugar and 1 tablespoon cinnamon all around. Then it is rolled up jelly-roll–style and baked with the hallahs. My children have this cinnamon bread for Friday breakfast.

INGREDIENTS

2 scant tablespoons or 2 envelopes
  active dried yeast
1½ cups warm water
1 teaspoon sugar
4 eggs
½ cup honey
½ cup vegetable oil
1½ teaspoons salt
8–9 cups flour
2 cups raisins (optional)
Sesame and/or poppy seeds

EQUIPMENT

Measuring cups
Measuring spoons
1 small bowl
Spoon
1 large bowl
Fork or wire whisk
Wooden spoon
Clean dish towel
Greased baking sheet or three
  9-inch round pans
Pastry brush

MAKES
3 LOAVES

Child with Adult: In a small bowl, stir together the yeast, 1 cup of the warm water, and the sugar. Set aside for 10 minutes and make sure it bubbles (this is called proofing the yeast).

Child: Beat 3 of the eggs with the honey. Add the remaining ½ cup warm water, oil, and salt. Add the yeast mixture, beating well with a spoon.

Child with Adult: Using 5 cups of the flour, add 1 cup at a time to your mixture, beating well with a wooden spoon after each addition. The dough will be sticky. If raisins are used, add them now. You can also use a food processor for this.

Child with Adult: Now add 2 more cups of flour, beating well with a wooden spoon until the dough leaves the sides of the bowl. Shake an additional 2 cups flour onto your work surface and knead the dough until almost all the flour is absorbed into it. Return it to the bowl. Cover with a towel and let rise for 1–2 hours, until it looks like it has grown to almost twice its size.

Child: When the dough has risen, punch it down. This means just that—hit the dough with your *very* clean fist.

Adult: Divide the dough into 3 equal parts, and divide each part into 3 again for braiding.

Child: Roll the dough into long ropes. Braid 3 together, as you would hair. Press down the ends. Leave the loaf long, or push the ends together into a circle. Place the loaves on the greased baking sheet or 9-inch round pans. Cover with a towel and let rise about 30 minutes more, until it is again almost twice its size.

Adult: Preheat oven to 350°.

Child: Brush the loaves with the remaining egg mixed with a little water. Sprinkle with sesame and/or poppy seeds.

Adult: Bake for 25 minutes, or until golden.

Note: To make a round hallah, take one ball of dough and roll it into a rope about 2 inches in diameter. Coil it from the outside in, letting each circle slightly overlap the one before.

VEGETARIAN CHOPPED LIVER

Just after the State of Israel was created, Israelis had little food to eat. Eggplant became a food that took on many forms. Fried, it sometimes tasted like the meat children could not get. Grated, it was used in cakes. But most often it was and still is roasted and turned into dips. This vegetarian chopped liver tastes like chopped liver, which in our grandparents' home in Poland was always part of the Friday night meal, eaten after the gefilte fish.

MAKES 2 CUPS

INGREDIENTS

1 medium eggplant

1 medium onion, minced

2 tablespoons (¼ stick) *pareve* margarine or butter

2 hard-boiled eggs

Salt and freshly ground pepper to taste

EQUIPMENT

Measuring spoons

Forks

Foil-lined baking sheet

Knife

Small frying pan

Food grinder or processor

Adult: Preheat oven to 450°.

Child: Pierce the eggplant with a fork.

Adult: Place the eggplant on a foil-lined baking sheet and cook about 20 minutes, or until soft. Remove from the oven, cool, and peel off the skin.

Adult: In a small frying pan, sauté half the minced onion in margarine or butter, turning occasionally with a fork.

Child with Adult: Grind the eggplant, fried and raw onions, and eggs in a food grinder or processor until they are the consistency of chopped liver.

Child: Add as much salt and pepper as you like. Refrigerate. Remove from the refrigerator 30 minutes before serving.

MATZAH BALL SOUP

Jewish chicken soup has achieved international status. Even doctors believe that the soothing properties of the boiled chicken can help bring down the fever from flu. Chicken soup has always been special, because slaughtering and eating a chicken was reserved for special days. Most of the time, the chickens were left to lay eggs. In Europe, our grandparents ate potato or mushroom-barley soup with a leftover meat bone during the week. Chicken soup was reserved for Friday nights or festive occasions. Ask your parents or grandparents if they remember when chickens were bought from the kosher butcher and then cooked with the feet attached (nails cut off, of course!).

CHICKEN ſOUP

INGREDIENTſ

1 5- or 6-pound hen or roasting
   chicken, cleaned
2 large celery stalks with leaves,
   chopped
2 large carrots, sliced in big
   chunks
1 onion, quartered
3 sprigs parsley
3 sprigs fresh or 1 teaspoon dried
   dill
Salt and pepper to taste

EQUIPMENT

Large pot with lid
Large spoon
Strainer
Knife

MAKEſ ABOUT 2 QUARTſ

Child with Adult: Wash the chicken with water and place in a pot. Cover with water.

Adult: Remove pot to stove, over high heat. Skim off the bubbling foam as it forms.

Child: Add the remaining ingredients, lower the heat, and simmer, half-covered, for at least 45 minutes, until the chicken seems done. The chicken will come away easily from the bone.

Adult: Adjust seasonings, letting the children judge the amounts. Pour the soup through a strainer to get a clear broth. Let cool; when the broth has completely cooled, skim off the fat and save it for the matzah balls.

Child: Remove the chicken meat from the bones, using your fingers. Cut up the meat for dinner or for a chicken salad. Of course, you're expected to nibble while you work!

Adult: Reheat the broth before serving.

MATZAH BALLS

In our house, matzah balls mean Friday night dinner or a Jewish holiday. Eyes light up. Maybe it's the soft texture, or it's the aroma of the soup combined with the mild taste of the matzah dumplings. You may be surprised to see that some of my menus suggest you follow what is basically chicken soup with a chicken or turkey dish—I assure you that it's children's idea of heaven.

INGREDIENTS

4 eggs (or 2 eggs and 2 whites), lightly beaten
4 tablespoons chicken fat or ½ stick melted *pareve* margarine
1 cup matzah meal
2 teaspoons salt
¼ cup hot water
12 cups salted water

EQUIPMENT

Measuring spoons
Measuring cups
Mixing bowl
Spoon
Large pot with lid
Slotted spoon

MAKES ABOUT 20

Child: Mix together the eggs and the chicken fat or margarine. Stir in the matzah meal and salt. Add the hot water. Cover and refrigerate for at least 1 hour.

Child: Form the matzah dough into balls the size of walnuts.

Child with Adult: In a large pot, bring the salted water to a boil. Add the matzah balls, cover, and cook for 20 minutes (don't even peek!). Remove with a slotted spoon and put in the simmering chicken broth just a few minutes before serving.

FRIDAY NIGHT POT ROAST

Sometimes what is easiest is most delicious. There is rarely a Friday night in my family without a pot roast. Originally this dish was a long-cooking way to make tough meat tender. If you can afford it, use brisket; otherwise, chuck roast will do just fine. Please save the leftovers to serve with noodles—my favorite leftover meal as a child. This is my mother's recipe.

INGREDIENTS

2 teaspoons salt
3 tablespoons brown sugar
1 cup chili sauce
1 cup white vinegar
2 cloves garlic, mashed
1 3-pound brisket, shoulder roast of beef, chuck roast, or end of steak
1 cup chopped celery leaves
2 onions, sliced
4 carrots, peeled and sliced
2 cups tomato juice

EQUIPMENT

Mixing bowl
Large ovenproof casserole with lid
Basting spoon

SERVES
6

Child: Mix together the salt, sugar, chili sauce, vinegar, and garlic (this is your marinade). Wash the meat and place it in the casserole. Pour the marinade over the meat and cover it with the celery leaves, onions, carrots, and tomato juice. Cover the casserole and put it in the refrigerator overnight.

Adult: Preheat oven to 325°.

Adult with Child: Roast, covered, for about 2 hours, basting often with the marinade. Remove cover and cook for 1 more hour, allowing approximately 1 hour per pound for roasting. Cool and refrigerate.

Adult with Child: When completely cool, skim off the fat, which will have congealed.

Adult: Slice the meat thin, reheat, and serve in the strained pan marinade.

KIDS' QUICKY KNISHES

In Eastern Europe children and adults got tired of potatoes every day— potato soup, boiled, baked, and mashed potatoes, and even potato skins. One way to change that monotony and to make a special treat was to wrap the potatoes in a dough. We call these knishes. Some people think the word *knish* comes from the Yiddish *knapen*, to pinch. You'll notice that after you have used your hand to cut the knishes you pinch the top to enclose them. Here's a recipe that my children love to make—and, more important, to eat.

INGREDIENTS

2 onions, more or less to taste
(optional, depending on how
much your children like—or
dislike—onions)

1 tablespoon vegetable oil

1¼ pounds russet (baking) potatoes

Salt to taste

2 large eggs

¼ cup chopped fresh parsley

½ teaspoon salt or to taste

Freshly ground pepper to taste

1 pound 1½ ounces prepared puff
pastry*

1 teaspoon water

EQUIPMENT

Sharp knife

Frying pan with cover

Potato peeler

Cooking pot

Potato masher

Rolling pin

Wax paper or pastry board

Greased baking sheet

Pastry brush

MAKES
ABOUT 18
KNISHES

Adult: Slice the onions. Slowly cook the onions in the oil in a skillet, covered, over a low heat. Let the onions "sweat" for about 20 minutes, or until they are soft. Then remove the cover and let fry over a medium heat until golden brown. Don't drain.

Child: Peel the potatoes and cut them in half. Put them in a large pot filled with cold water and salt to taste.

Adult: Bring potatoes to a boil, then turn the heat down, and cook until soft, about 15 minutes. Drain and cool for 5 minutes. Take the prepared puff pastry from the refrigerator and let sit for about 20 minutes.

Child with Adult: Using a potato masher, mash the potatoes and add one of the eggs, the parsley, salt, and pepper. Add the onions with the oil (if using) and mix well with your hands. Set aside while preparing the dough.

* Pepperidge Farm makes a kosher puff pastry.

Child with Adult: Take one sheet of dough and roll out with a rolling pin on wax paper or on a pastry board until about ⅛ inch thick. Spread one-half of the filling (about 1½ cups) onto approximately one-third of the dough, leaving a 1-inch border. Holding on to the wax paper, roll up the dough like a jelly roll. Using the side of your hand like a knife, divide the roll into 2-inch knishes. Then pinch the open ends shut. Repeat with the remaining sheet of prepared puff pastry. Place the knishes, flat side down, on a greased baking sheet, leaving a 2-inch space between each.

Adult: Preheat oven to 375°.

Child: Mix the remaining egg with 1 teaspoon water. Brush the tops with the egg wash and bake for 25–30 minutes or until golden brown.

TURKEY TENDERS

Believe it or not, there is more turkey eaten in Israel per capita than in any other country in the world. Second, of course, is the United States. And, the most popular way to eat it is in *schnitzels*. The word for turkey in Hebrew is *hodoo*. *Hodoo* is the Hebrew name for the country India. They say that the early Americans thought the turkey came from Turkey and so they called it turkey. Perhaps Israelis thought the bird came from India.

You could make this Israeli style like *schnitzels,* but my children prefer these tenders. I have added toasted wheat germ to this recipe. It gives it an added crunch and is healthful too!

INGREDIENTS

1 whole turkey breast or 2 chicken
  breasts, skinned and boned
1 large egg
2 tablespoons warm water
3 tablespoons vegetable oil
1 teaspoon oregano
Salt and freshly ground pepper to
  taste
1 cup cornflake crumbs
3 tablespoons toasted wheat germ

EQUIPMENT

Sharp knife
Whisk or fork
2 soup bowls
Greased baking sheet

SERVES 4-6

Adult: Cut the turkey or chicken breasts into ½-inch by 3-inch strips.

Child: Beat the egg. Then mix it with the warm water, oil, oregano, and salt and pepper in a wide soup bowl. Mix the cornflake crumbs and the wheat germ in a second bowl. Dip the turkey strips into the egg mixture and then the cornflake–wheat-germ mixture. When you have done them all, place them on a greased baking sheet and put them in the refrigerator for a few hours.

Adult: Preheat oven to 350°. Bake the turkey tenders for 30 minutes, or until golden, or fry in a slight amount of additional oil until golden on each side.

PRETZEL BAGELS . . . OR BAGEL PRETZELS

Once I took my children to a factory in the Amish country in Pennsylvania where they made pretzels by hand. The pretzel baker told us that pretzels, a cousin of the bagel—not boiled, just baked—were originally rings put together to form a figure eight. So why not call them pretzel bagels . . . or bagel pretzels. This is a recipe my son, David, used in nursery school to make pretzels which the children would sell at an Israeli *shouk,* or marketplace.

INGREDIENTS

1 package or 1 scant tablespoon
  dry yeast
1 teaspoon honey
½ cup warm water
1 teaspoon salt
1 cup all-purpose flour
1 egg with water for wash, beaten
  lightly
Kosher salt
  or
Ground cinnamon and sugar

EQUIPMENT

Mixing bowls
Measuring cups
Measuring spoons
Eggbeater or whisk
Greased baking sheet

MAKES 4

Adult: Preheat oven to 425°.

Adult with Child: Dissolve the yeast and sugar in the water. In another bowl combine the salt and flour. Stir in the yeast mixture and add more flour if necessary to make it sticky but not too wet.

Child: Knead for 5 to 10 minutes. This is great fun. You can do this the proper way, using the heel of your hand to press and then gathering up the dough in your fingers, or you can treat it like Play-Doh, squeezing and squishing it as you wish. Break it off in 4 small pieces. Using the palm of your hand, roll out the dough into a long cylinder like a snake, about 8–10 inches long. Then twist it into a circle and place it on a greased baking sheet. You can also make Hebrew letters, Hebrew names, or figure-eight pretzels from the dough. To make a pretzel, take both ends of the snake, lift them up, and cross them in the center of the circle of dough. Brush it with the beaten egg and sprinkle with the kosher salt, or you may want to sprinkle it with cinnamon sugar.

Adult: Bake in the oven for 10–15 minutes. Remove to a drying rack and serve. Yummy!

CREAM CHEESE OR SPINACH BUREKAS

In Jerusalem, Saturday morning means burekas, little triangular pastries filled with cheese or spinach, made the day before and eaten by children with hot chocolate and by adults with strong coffee. Burekas are easy to make and can be prepared ahead for snacks. They can even be served at adult cocktail parties and passed around by the children, who are proud to claim credit for them.

INGREDIENTS

½ cup farmer's cheese

1 large egg, lightly beaten

1 cup finely grated cheddar cheese

2 ounces cream cheese

⅛ teaspoon salt

Pinch ground nutmeg

Pinch ground white pepper

8 sheets fillo dough, cut into
   3-inch strips

½ cup (1 stick) butter, melted

EQUIPMENT

Measuring cups

Measuring spoons

Mixing bowl

Fork

Pastry brush

Spoon

Pancake turner

Greased baking sheet

MAKES ABOUT 48

SPINACH FILLING:

INGREDIENTS

10 ounces chopped fresh spinach

1 large egg, lightly beaten

1 cup finely grated Swiss or cheddar cheese or cream cheese

2 tablespoons feta cheese

Dash of ground nutmeg

Generous sprinkle of pepper

EQUIPMENT

Measuring cup

Measuring spoons

Saucepan with lid

Strainer

Large spoon

Chopping knife

Wooden bowl

To make cream cheese burekas:

Adult: Preheat oven to 350°.

Child: In a bowl, mash the farmer's cheese with a fork until crumbly. Mix in the egg, cheddar cheese, cream cheese, salt, nutmeg, and white pepper. Blend well.

Child: Brush each fillo strip with butter and spread 1 teaspoon of the cheese mixture in a corner. Fold over like a flag to make a triangle, fold again to make a square, then a third time to make a triangle. Using a pancake turner, place on a greased baking sheet. Brush the top with butter. Repeat with the remaining filling and the remaining fillo dough.

Adult: Bake for about 15 minutes, until golden. Eat immediately, or refrigerate and reheat next morning for Shabbat breakfast.

To make spinach filling:

Child: Wash the spinach well, rinsing two or three times. Place in a saucepan with just the water that clings to the leaves after washing. Cover tightly and cook over medium heat until tender, about 4 or 5 minutes. Remove the spinach, place it in a strainer, and press out the remaining water with the back of a spoon. Chop fine in a wooden bowl. Mix well with the egg, cheeses, nutmeg, and pepper.

Follow directions for filling and baking cream cheese burekas.

CHILDREN'S CHOLENT

When our children's grandmother was a little girl in Poland, her favorite Sabbath dish was cholent, the long-cooking stew put in the oven and sealed on Friday before the Sabbath began and then eaten on Saturday for lunch. Her favorite part of the dish was the thinly sliced potatoes her mother put on top. It is great fun for children to make a cholent and see the result after it has cooked all night long. Make sure they are there when you open the cover.

Let the Sabbath during Sukkot be the first time of the year you serve cholent—a one-dish meal is very easy to carry out to the *sukkah*.

INGREDIENTS

1 cup dried lima or kidney beans
2 onions, cut in quarters
2 tablespoons (¼ stick) plus ⅓ cup (⅔ stick) *pareve* margarine
3 pounds chuck
Salt and freshly ground pepper to taste
2 cloves garlic
6 carrots, sliced
2 tablespoons molasses
1 package onion-soup mix
6 medium potatoes, sliced thin
1 cup self-rising flour
2 tablespoons ice water

EQUIPMENT

Bowl
Measuring cups
Measuring spoons
Frying pan
Pan for browning meat
Large ovenproof casserole with lid
Strainer or colander
Teakettle

SERVES AT LEAST 10

Child: The night before starting to prepare the cholent, put the lima or

soak beans overnight

**melt margarine
in pan**

sauté onions

season meat

brown meat in pan

combine in casserole

drain beans & add

add carrots

add molasses

add onion soup mix

**top with sliced
potatoes**

**cover with
boiling water**

seal lid with dough

cook overnight

kidney beans in a bowl and cover them with water. Let them soak overnight

Adult with Child: Sauté the onions in a frying pan in 2 tablespoons of the margarine.

Child: Salt and pepper the meat and rub in the garlic.

Child with Adult: Brown the meat in the frying pan on top of the stove. Put it and the onions in a large, heavy casserole.

Child: Drain the beans. Add them, along with the carrots and molasses, to the casserole. Sprinkle with the onion-soup mix. Then carefully add the sliced potatoes in a layer over the top.

Adult: Bring a teakettle of water to a boil. Cover the cholent with the boiling water.

Child with Adult: Make a dough from the remaining ⅓ cup margarine, the flour, a dash of salt, and the ice water. Spread the dough all around the rim of the casserole like putty, and put on the lid, sticking it to the dough to make sure no air gets in while cooking. Bake in a 250° oven for about 12 hours. Open and eat!

MANDELBROT

When my husband was growing up, his mother always made special cookies for the Sabbath. She would first bake the cookies, usually called mandelbrot from *mandel* (almond) and *brot* (bread), like a loaf cake, then slice them and bake them again. We've added chocolate chips to our modern version.

INGREDIENTS

1 cup (2 sticks) unsalted *pareve* margarine or butter, softened
1 cup plus 2 teaspoons sugar
4 eggs
1 teaspoon vanilla
½ cup orange juice
4 cups unbleached all-purpose flour
2 teaspoons baking powder
1 teaspoon salt
2 cups chocolate chips
1 cup grated coconut
½ cup chopped almonds or pecans (optional)
¼ teaspoon ground cinnamon

EQUIPMENT

Measuring cups
Measuring spoons
Mixing bowls
Fork
Hand beater or large spoon
3 bread pans
Knife
Baking sheets

MAKES 3 LOAVES OR 36 COOKIES

Adult: Preheat oven to 350°.

Child: Using a fork, cream together the margarine and 1 cup sugar. In a separate bowl, using a hand beater or large spoon, beat the eggs well.

Combine them with the margarine and sugar mixture, vanilla, and orange juice.

Child: In another bowl, mix together the flour, baking powder, and salt. Add this to the margarine mixture. Mix well.

Child: Blend in the chocolate chips, coconut, and nuts. Grease and flour 3 bread pans, put the dough in them, and bake for 30–40 minutes, until done. Cool and cut carefully into ½-inch slices.

Adult: Turn up oven to 400°.

Child with Adult: Arrange the mandelbrot slices on baking sheets. Mix the cinnamon with the remaining 2 teaspoons sugar and sprinkle over the top. Brown in the oven for a few minutes, until golden.

Note: You can also use a food processor for this recipe.

HAVDALAH

Havdalah, the ceremony marking the close of the Sabbath at sunset, is one of the nicest aspects of Shabbat for children. It reflects the real "spice and spirit" of the Sabbath. As soon as the first stars are seen in the sky, the Havdalah candle is lit. As opposed to the two separate candles ushering in the Sabbath, the Havdalah candle has at least two and usually three entwined wicks which come together to strengthen it, just as we enter the new week with the experience of Shabbat strengthening us. You can make your own Havdalah candles. Just use 3 long, very thin candles. Dip them in hot water and braid them together, crimping them with foil at the bottom. (Younger children can also do this with stick licorice.) This is a project where older children can help younger ones.

Our grandmother's superstition suggests that when the candle is lit, it be held high in the direction of a daughter, to ensure that she'll find a tall husband.

After the candle is lit, there is a blessing over the wine, which symbolizes joy. Then the spices are blessed. Make this seasonal in your home. Pick flowers or aromatic herbs from your garden in the summer, and let your children select spices from a health-food store's open bins in winter. The spices, most often cinnamon and cloves, symbolize the spiritual riches of the Sabbath and are sniffed before replacing them in the receptacle, in a child's case a matchbox, film container, or pill bottle. A child can also pierce an orange or an apple with cloves (see page 49). These spices are to cheer the soul—so saddened by the departure of the Sabbath.

ROSH HASHANAH

ROSH HASHANAH DINNER

Round Hallah*
Apples Dipped in Honey
Matzah Ball Soup*
Orange Chicken*
Rice
Carrot Tsimmes*
Easy Pear Strudel*

ROSH HASHANAH LUNCH

Round Hallah*
Golden Harvest Tsimmes*
Baked Apples*

ROSH HASHANAH

● ● ● ● ●

Rosh Hashanah, literally "head of the year," is the Jewish New Year. To our family, it means not only the beginning of school, but the beginning of a new yearly cycle. We like to think of the symbolism of the food at this time of year. No dark foods—only bright fresh oranges, carrots, honey, apples. Circles mean a good year all year round. We shape our hallah into a circle for Rosh Hashanah, sometimes adding golden raisins for an even sweeter year. We always start our meal with apples dipped in honey.

Our dinner on the eve of the holiday is a rather hurried affair, between coming home from school and work and rushing off to synagogue. The luncheon after Rosh Hashanah morning services is our time for a real feast.

CARROT TSIMMES

● ● ● ● ●

The carrots in this recipe resemble coins. They make it a triply symbolic recipe for the New Year—round, brightly colored, and sweet. What better way for our children to eat vegetables!

INGREDIENTS
1 pound carrots
1 8-ounce can crushed pineapple
½ cup water
½ cup orange juice
½ teaspoon ground ginger
½ teaspoon salt
6 ounces pitted prunes

EQUIPMENT
Measuring cups
Measuring spoons
Vegetable peeler
Saucepan with lid
Plastic knife
Spoon

SERVES
6

Child: Peel the carrots.

Adult: Cook carrots in boiling salted water for about 20 minutes, or in the microwave, until soft. Let cool.

Child: Slice the carrots with a plastic knife into round circles. Mix them with the crushed pineapple, water, orange juice, ginger, salt, and prunes. Simmer them, covered, on top of the stove for about 15 minutes.

IJRAELI COIN CARROT JALAD

● ● ● ● ●

Here is an Israeli carrot salad that I learned to make years ago when I lived in Jerusalem. It's delicious to eat any time during the year, but especially at Rosh Hashanah when we welcome the sweet New Year.

INGREDIENTJ

1 pound carrots
½ teaspoon salt or to taste
¼ cup orange juice
2 tablespoons candied ginger, diced
Handful of raisins
2 tablespoons chopped fresh parsley

EQUIPMENT

Vegetable peeler
6-cup saucepan
Paper towel
Plastic knife
Measuring cup
Measuring spoons
Serving bowl

JERVEJ 4–6

Child: Peel the carrots.

Adult: Add the 6 cups cold water to the saucepan. Bring to a boil and add salt. Put in the carrots and let simmer, uncovered, for about 10 to 15 minutes, or until tender. Drain and pat dry with a paper towel.

Child: When the carrots are cool enough to handle, slice them in rounds about ¼ inch thick. Choose a pretty serving bowl. Place the carrots in the bowl. Cover with the orange juice and sprinkle with the ginger, raisins, and chopped parsley.

Adult: Cover bowl with plastic wrap and refrigerate for at least 6 hours, turning occasionally so that the flavors can blend.

ORANGE CHICKEN

● ● ● ● ●

The fun for the children comes from sticking the orange into the chicken and then seeing the surprise on their father's face when he carves it: the orange pops out and slides across the table!

INGREDIENTS
1 4- to 5-pound chicken
1 orange
1 cup orange juice
½ cup chicken broth
1 teaspoon salt
1 teaspoon pepper
1 teaspoon ground ginger
¼ cup honey

EQUIPMENT
Measuring cups
Measuring spoons
Roasting pan
Mixing bowl
Spoon or baster
Plastic knife

SERVES
6–8

Adult: Preheat oven to 350°. Clean and dry the chicken. Place in a roasting pan, breast side down.

Child: Wash the orange in water and place in the cavity of the chicken. Mix together the orange juice, chicken broth, salt, pepper, and ginger, and pour the mixture over the chicken. Roast, uncovered, for 30 minutes.

Adult: Remove the chicken from the oven. Turn it over.

Child: Using a spoon or plastic knife, smear the chicken with the honey.

Adult: Baste with juices from the pan. Return the chicken to the oven and roast 20 minutes more, or until the drumstick moves easily.

SORT OF SEPHARDIC SWEET POTATOES AND SQUASH

●　●　●　●　●

Sephardic Jews from Turkey, Greece, Morocco, and other countries of the Mediterranean region say seven special blessings over seven different symbolic foods at their Rosh Hashanah dinner. Five of these blessings are over vegetables—apples (candied or dipped in sugar or honey), leeks, beet greens or spinach, dates, and zucchini or squash. These blessings symbolize their hopes for the New Year. Many of these Jews trace their ancestors back to Spain, which is called *Sepharad* in the Bible. Over the centuries, the Sephardic Jews took advantage of the abundance of vegetables available in the Mediterranean countries, often throughout the year. Among these vegetables are sweet potatoes and squash, great favorites of my family. The special blessing you can say over your sweet potatoes and squash at the beginning of your Rosh Hashanah dinner goes like this:

Yehi ratzon mi-le-faneha Adonai Eloheinu ve-lo-hei avoteinu she-tik-rah ro-a gezar dinenu ve-yi-karehu lefa-neha za-hee-yo-teinu.

May it be thy will, Lord our God and God of our fathers, that you should tear up any evil decree and let only our merits be read before You.

INGREDIENTS
1 pound acorn or butternut squash
1 pound sweet potatoes or yams
2 tablespoons vegetable oil
¼ cup dried cranberries or cherries
2 tablespoons brown sugar
1 teaspoon ground cinnamon

EQUIPMENT
Vegetable peeler
Sharp paring knife
Wooden spoon
Frying pan
Mixing bowl
Aluminum foil
Oblong casserole dish (about 9 by 13 inches)

SERVES
6

Adult: Preheat oven to 375°. Peel the squash.

Child: Peel the sweet potatoes or yams. Then carefully cut both the sweet potatoes and squash into 1-inch cubes. Place most of the oil in the casserole. Add the sweet potatoes and bake, covered with aluminum foil, about 20 minutes.

Adult: Take out the hot dish from the oven and carefully remove the foil.

Child: Add the squash and the cranberries or cherries. Sprinkle the sugar and cinnamon on top and dribble with the remaining oil.

Adult: Bake uncovered at 375° for 30–35 minutes, or until well browned. Serve with roast chicken or pot roast.

Note: If your family likes onions, add one, sautéed in the oil until soft, to the sweet potatoes before baking.

POMEGRANATES

One of the most biblical of fruits is the pomegranate, which legend says has 613 seeds in it, the same as the number of commandments in the Bible. My daughter Daniela counted 498 in one. Some people think that the tree of life was a pomegranate tree. At Rosh Hashanah the pomegranate symbolizes our wishes for abundance in the New Year. The word itself in French, *pomme grenate,* means "apple with seeds." When our family visits Israel our favorite tree to look at—and to taste—in summer and early fall is the pomegranate. At one vegetarian *moshav* in Israel we saw the individual fruits carefully covered in plastic bags to ward off unwanted birds and bugs, an ecological way of ensuring good fruit and certainly something not done in biblical times! In our family, we like pomegranates in a variety of ways. We eat the seeds individually as a snack, we sprinkle them on cereal, we put them over grapefruit and orange sections in fruit cups, and we drink the juice alone or mixed with grapefruit and orange juice.

As far as I am concerned, Jews from Iran know more about pomegranates than anyone else. They have taught me how to peel a pomegranate and how Persian Jewish children drink the juice straight from the fruit or, to be more correct, they suck the juice out from the fruit. We have added a straw and call it Pomegranate Punch. It is a big hit with my children and their friends. Try it.

PEELING A POMEGRANATE

● ● ● ● ●

INGREDIENT
1 smooth, red pomegranate

EQUIPMENT
1 sharp paring knife
1 small or 1 huge mixing bowl
Sieve or strainer

Adult: Using a sharp knife, score the top of the pomegranate where there are natural humps, making 1-inch-long incisions.

Child: Carefully peel off the pomegranate skin and even more carefully remove the seeds with your fingers to a small bowl. Or, to ensure that no squirts of pomegranate juice spot your house, fill a huge mixing bowl with cold water. Once you have scored the pomegranate place it in the bowl. Roll up your sleeves and grasp the pomegranate under the water. Remove the skin, then the seeds, which will fall to the bottom of the bowl. Once you have finished, drain off the water, and you will have plump, delicious pomegranate seeds. Eat them as is or make juice from them.

Adult with Child: To make juice, place the pomegranate seeds in a sieve over a small mixing bowl. Using your hands, press as hard as you can to extract the juice. Be careful to wash your hands right away afterward.

PERSIAN POMEGRANATE PUNCH

● ● ● ● ●

INGREDIENT
1 pomegranate

EQUIPMENT
1 shish kebab skewer
1 straw

SERVES 1

Child: Take a smooth pomegranate and roll it on a countertop until all the crunchy sounds stop. Bear down as much as you can without breaking the skin. You will have to do this over all the pomegranate. It will take a while but it is great fun. Once it is soft all around and there is no crunchiness left, give the pomegranate to an adult.

Adult: Placing the pomegranate on the table, take a shish kebab skewer and gently make a hole in the pomegranate. You may have to quickly suck out some of the juice. Then take a straw and insert it into the pomegranate.

Child: Drink the pomegranate juice through the straw. It is delicious. It will take a few seconds for the juice to come into the straw but it is worth waiting for!

Note: This is also a good way to extract juice for recipes.

BAKED APPLES

● ● ● ● ●

One of our children's favorite desserts is baked apples, which they like to make themselves. They improvise with the spices and garnishes. Baked apples, pomegranates, plums, or figs can be used for the first fruits of the New Year.

Whichever new fruit you use, say the following prayer:

Baruch atah Adonai Eloheinu melech ha-olam, shehecheyanu, ve-kiyemanu, ve-higianu, laz-man ha-zeh.
Blessed art Thou, O Lord our God, who hast kept us alive, sustained us, and enabled us to reach this special day.

INGREDIENTS
6 apples
6 1-inch cinnamon sticks
Raisins (optional)
4 tablespoons honey
½ cup cider
2 tablespoons (¼ stick) margarine
  or butter

EQUIPMENT
Measuring spoons
Measuring cup
Apple corer
Knife
Baking pan

SERVES
6

Adult: Preheat oven to 350°.

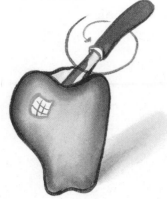

Child: Carefully core each apple, letting an adult show you how to use an apple corer. Peel away the skin from the top part of the apple. Put the apples in the baking pan. Stick a 1-inch cinnamon stick in each apple where you removed the core. Sprinkle with raisins and dab with honey. Pour the cider in the core hole. Dot the tops of the apples with margarine or butter.

Adult: Bake for 30 minutes, or until soft.

EASY PEAR STRUDEL

• • • • •

Foods such as stuffed cabbage, stuffed grape leaves, and stuffed strudel have the same significance at Rosh Hashanah and the harvest period—a wish for a new, full year ahead. Knowing how much children like to play with fillo dough, we make this recipe for our luncheon guests at the New Year.

INGREDIENTS
2 Bartlett pears
¼ cup sugar
¼ cup raisins
2 tablespoons chopped nuts
½ teaspoon ground cinnamon
Grated rind of 1 lemon
4 sheets fillo dough
½ cup (1 stick) butter or margarine, melted
¼ cup fine dry bread crumbs or matzah meal
Confectioners' sugar

EQUIPMENT
Measuring cups
Measuring spoons
Paring knife or vegetable peeler
Knife
Mixing bowl
Clean cloth
Pastry brush
Greased jelly roll pan
Tea strainer

SERVES 4–6

Adult: Peel one pear, showing the child how. Then let the child peel the second. Cut into bite-size pieces, removing the core.

Child: Mix the pears with the sugar, raisins, nuts, cinnamon, and lemon rind.

Adult: Preheat oven to 375°.

Child with Adult: Take one fillo sheet and spread out on a cloth on a flat surface. Brush with the butter or margarine and sprinkle with 1 tablespoon of the bread crumbs. Place a second fillo sheet on top. Brush with butter and sprinkle with bread crumbs or matzah meal. Place half the pear mixture at one end of the fillo sheets, covering about 2 inches and leaving a 1-inch border. Starting with that end, carefully roll, jelly roll fashion, ending with the seam on the bottom. Brush the top with more butter and place in a greased jelly roll pan.

Repeat with the remaining filling and the remaining fillo dough.

Adult: Bake for 35 minutes, or until golden.

Child: Just before serving, sprinkle with confectioners' sugar, using a tea strainer. Cut and serve warm.

YOM KIPPUR

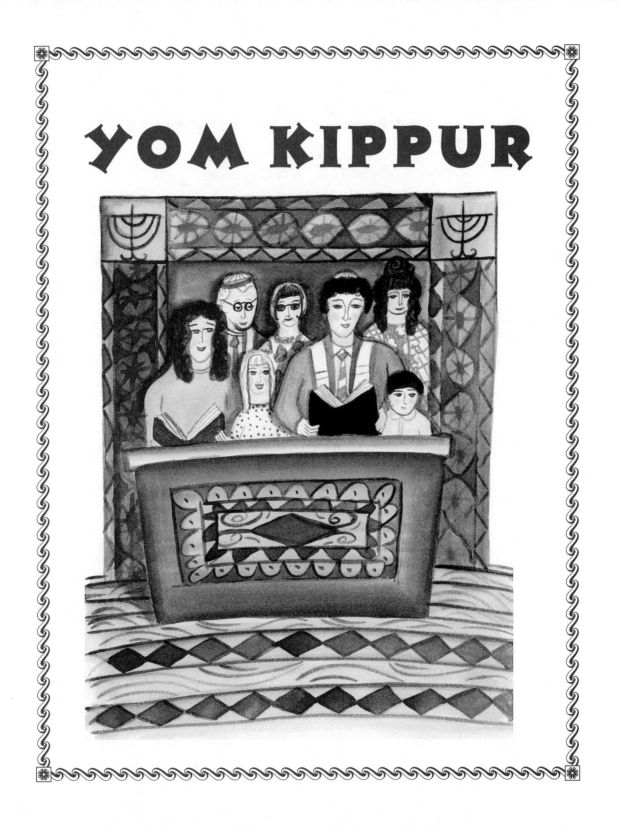

YEMENITE DINNER BEFORE THE FAST

Kubbanah*
Yemenite High Holy Day Soup*
Apple-Honey Cupcakes*

EASTERN EUROPEAN DINNER BEFORE THE FAST

Kreplakh* in Chicken Soup*
Friday Night Pot Roast*
Rice
Baked Apples*

BREAK THE FAST MENU

Greek Lemonade*
Apples Dipped in Honey
Round Hallah*
Bagels*
Apple and Cream Cheese Spread*
Fruit Kugel*
Cucumber-Yoghurt Salad*
Apple-Honey Cupcakes*

YOM KIPPUR

Yom Kippur, the Day of Atonement, is a day of fasting and repentance. The holiest day of the year is not a time to think about cooking—but our family does, especially to break the fast. The children always help.

In this country, a milk meal is usually served to break the fast, beginning with coffee, tea, or brandy and a sweet—sometimes an apple dipped in honey or a piece of honey cake—followed by herring or another salty food. From there on, it is up to the imagination or the background of the hosts. Russian Jews often make schnecken; Moroccans, fijuelas (deep-fried pastries oozing with honey); Syrians and Egyptians make a cardamom cake, and Yemenites a ginger cake. Quinces, pomegranates, watermelon, or other seasonal fruits are also served. It is becoming more and more traditional in this country to serve a glorified brunch with bagels, lox, cream cheese, herring, kugel, and such.

Once, when I lived in Jerusalem, I started the fast of Yom Kippur with Yemenite Jews. Some say Yemenite Jews separated from the ancient Israelites when wandering for forty years in the desert, veering off and heading south to the Arabian Peninsula, near Ethiopia. Others say the Queen of Sheba brought the Yemenites back with her from Palestine. Even though Yemenite Jews were separated from the Jews of Europe and the Middle East for three thousand years, they still observe many of the same customs, including bread to start each holiday meal. One such bread is kubbanah, which is kneaded for a long period of time and then baked in hot embers because the Yemenites did not have the kinds of ovens we know today. I use a Dutch oven instead.

KUBBANAH

INGREDIENTS

1 tablespoon dry yeast
1 cup lukewarm water
1 tablespoon sugar
4 cups flour
1 tablespoon salt
½ cup vegetable oil

EQUIPMENT

Measuring spoons
Measuring cups
Large mixing bowl
Spoon
Clean dish towel
Dutch oven

SERVES 8–10

Child: In a bowl, mix together the yeast, the water, and the sugar, and make sure it bubbles. Then gradually add the flour and salt, kneading until well mixed. Cover with a clean towel and let rise for about 2 hours.

Adult: Pour oil into the Dutch oven over *low* heat on the stove. Flatten the dough and put into the pot. Cook, covered, for 1½ hours. Turn the kubbanah after about 1 hour, or when the top is done enough to turn. Serve hot, dipped in soup or hot sauce.

YEMENITE HIGH HOLY DAY SOUP

My mother-in-law remembers the *kapparah* tradition in Poland. Early in the morning of the day prior to Yom Kippur, a fowl was whirled about her head, while she thought about turning over a new leaf. Her father would whirl a rooster, her mother a hen, and her brothers and sisters a pullet or a cockerel. The ceremony was repeated for each child. She was always frightened by the fluttering feathers. After the whirling, her mother would race to the *shohet* and have the fowls ritually slaughtered to make food for the meal before the fast. All the fowls would be cooked, and any extras given to bachelor relatives or to the poor. Chicken soup would be made for the kreplakh and the boiled chicken eaten as a mild main dish.

Yemenite Jews also eat chicken before the fast of Yom Kippur, but much earlier in the morning, at about 10:30. Their soup is dipped with the kubbanah bread.

The *kapparah* offering is an Eastern European custom.

INGREDIENTS

3 celery stalks, cut into 2-inch pieces

1 medium zucchini, peeled and cubed

3 carrots, cut into 3-inch pieces

1 large tomato, almost quartered but not cut apart at bottom

3 potatoes, peeled and diced, kept in cold water

3 pounds beef shoulder, ribs, or stew meat (fat removed)

3 pieces (about 2 pounds) marrow bones

1 3-pound chicken, cleaned and quartered

Up to 5 quarts water

10–12 cloves garlic, unpeeled

9 small white onions

1 large white turnip, quartered but unpeeled

4 leeks or 8 green onions, coarsely cut

1 small bunch fresh parsley or fresh coriander, woody stems trimmed away

Salt to taste

1 tablespoon hawayij (Yemenite spices), or to taste

EQUIPMENT

Storage cups for refrigerating

Covered soup kettle

Large slotted spoon

SERVES 10–12

Note: Making a children's version of hawayij is a great introduction to Middle Eastern spices. Take the children to a spice store where they can pick out the spices themselves. Hawayij is basically a combination of cumin, coriander (omit if using fresh), curry powder, ginger, black pepper, and turmeric. Add spices according to your children's tolerance for strong and unusual flavors. You can omit them altogether if you wish.

Child: Store the celery, zucchini, carrots, tomato, and potatoes in separate covered containers in the refrigerator until you need them the next day. The potatoes must be in cold water or they will turn a terrible gray color.

Adult with Child: Place the beef and chicken in a large kettle with enough water to cover them. Bring to a boil, lower the heat, and simmer, until a froth forms. Remove the meat and bones and discard the water. Clean the kettle.

Child: Put the beef and bones back in the kettle and cover with fresh water. Bring to a boil again. Lower the heat and add the unpeeled garlic cloves (by being left in their skins, they won't soften in cooking). Add the onions, turnip, and leeks or green onions. Cook, covered, about 1½ hours, or until the meat seems fairly tender.

Adult: Remove the marrow bones, add the chicken, cover, and simmer another 20 minutes. Let cool and refrigerate overnight.

Child: Bring the soup to a boil. Add the celery, zucchini, carrots, tomato, and potatoes. Lower the heat, cover, and simmer another 20 minutes. Just before serving, add the parsley or coriander, salt, and hawayij, and cook, covered, for a few minutes.

Adult: Remove the garlic cloves. Adjust the seasonings.

Eat by dipping bread into the soup, scooping up the meat and vegetables and/or the sauce.

APPLE "EMBALMED" WITH CLOVES

When my father was a boy in southern Germany, he started fasting at Yom Kippur when he was bar mitzvah. Days before the fast, he took an apple and "embalmed" it with cloves. He brought it with him to the synagogue and sniffed it whenever he felt that he might faint from hunger. Once I attended a North African synagogue in Annecy, France, at Yom Kippur. Children held quince rubbed with cloves. An apple "embalmed" with cloves can also be used at Havdalah to let the smells of the Sabbath linger on.

INGREDIENTS
1 red apple
1 handful of cloves

Child: Taking the apple in one hand, pierce it at 1-inch intervals with whole cloves.

GREEK LEMONADE

After the final blowing of the shofar, Jews return home to break the fast. Customs differ from household to household around the world. What is essential is that the drink be thirst-quenching. In the United States, adults often drink orange juice, brandy, coffee, or hot tea. In Greece, depending on what area they come from, Jews sip drinks made from yoghurt, almonds, pomegranates, black cherries, pumpkin seeds, or lemons.

INGREDIENTS

6 lemons, at room temperature
Sugar to taste
Water
Fresh mint to taste

EQUIPMENT

Knife
Fork
Measuring cup
Spoon

MAKES
2 CUPS

Adult: Cut the lemons in half.

Child: Using a fork, pierce the inside of the lemon. If you are right-handed, place the lemon in that hand. Place your left hand palm up over a measuring cup. Squeeze the lemon with your right hand, letting the juice pour through the fingers of your left hand to catch all the seeds. Dilute the lemon juice with water and add as much sugar as you wish.

Serve cold in tall glasses which have been frosted in the freezer. Add long sprigs of mint for color.

KREPLAKH

Kreplakh—often called Jewish wonton—are traditional for the meal before the fast. Children love making noodles. Kreplakh are also eaten on Simhat Torah and Purim. Here is our recipe, which often turns out in varied shapes—no matter, they taste good and we feel great making them ourselves.

INGREDIENTS

MEAT FILLING:

1 small onion, chopped

¾ pound ground meat, cooked

1 egg

Salt and pepper to taste

NOODLE DOUGH:

3 eggs

¾ teaspoon salt

2 tablespoons water

2 cups all-purpose flour

EQUIPMENT

Frying pan

Wooden spoon

Mixing bowl

Fork

Clean moist towel

Rolling pin

Knife

Measuring spoon

Large pot with boiling water

Slotted spoon

MAKES ABOUT 60

To make the filling:

Adult: Sauté the onion with the ground meat. Pour off excess fat. Let cool slightly.

Child: Mix the meat mixture with the egg. Add as much salt and pepper as you like.

sauté onion & meat

add egg, salt & pepper

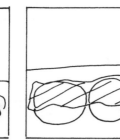

beat eggs

add salt, water & flour

knead dough well

cover with towel

roll out dough & cut

**add meat mixture
& fold**

drop into boiling water

remove with slotted spoon

serve & eat!

To make the noodles:

Child with Adult: Using a fork, lightly beat the eggs. Add salt, water, and enough flour to make a medium-soft dough. Knead well and quickly by hand. Divide the dough into 2 balls. Cover with a moist towel.

Adult, then Child: Working quickly, roll out one ball of dough very thin with a rolling pin and cut into 6 strips, each 1½ inches wide. Then cut into pieces 1½ inches square.

Child: Place ½ teaspoon meat mixture on each square. Fold into a triangle and press the edges together firmly, using flour to make it stick. Leave as is, or press together two of the ends. Repeat with the second ball of dough.

Child: Drop kreplakh into boiling water and cook, uncovered, for 15 minutes. Remove with a slotted spoon.

APPLE-HONEY CUPCAKES

For East European Jews, honey, a reminder of hope for a sweet future, is essential to bring in the New Year.

INGREDIENTS

¼ cup vegetable oil
¾ cup honey
2 eggs, well beaten
2 cups sifted all-purpose flour
1 teaspoon baking powder
1 teaspoon baking soda
1 teaspoon salt
2 cups coarsely grated raw apples
1 teaspoon ground cinnamon
½ teaspoon ground nutmeg
½ teaspoon ground allspice
¼ teaspoon ground cloves
⅔ cup chopped walnuts

EQUIPMENT

Measuring cups
Measuring spoons
Mixing bowls
Wooden spoon
Sifter
Paper muffin cups
Muffin tins

MAKES
18

Adult: Preheat oven to 350°.

Child: Mix the oil with the honey. Mix in the eggs. Sift together the flour, baking powder, baking soda, and salt. Mix the grated apples with the spices and nuts. Add a little of the flour mixture to the egg mixture, then a little grated apple, then some more flour mixture, and so on, until all the flour and apple mixtures are used up.

Child: Place the dough in paper muffin cups in muffin pans, ⅔ full. Bake for about 20 minutes, until done. Let cool, and serve plain or smeared with honey.

SUKKOT

SUKKOT HARVEST MENU

Vegetarian Chopped Liver*
Sukkot Stuffed Vegetables*
Zucchini Bread*

SUKKOT SABBATH LUNCH

Pasta with Vegetables and Pine Nuts*
Green Salad
Apple-Honey Cupcakes*

SUKKOT

The fall holiday of Sukkot commemorates the Jews' wandering in the wilderness after fleeing Egypt. For forty years they lived in *sukkot* (booths) in the desert. Sukkot also marks the harvest time when the farmers gather the last fruits from the fields and vineyards. In ancient Israel, farmers would build and live in little huts—also called *sukkot*—in their fields during the harvest to save time.

For the eight days of the Sukkot harvest, foods are served in outdoor booths, so it's a good time to think in terms of one-dish meals. Make this the first time of the year to prepare a cholent. The booth, or *sukkah,* has an open top to let the sky show through and is decorated with seasonal fruits and vegetables.

Our first *sukkah* was made of bamboo poles from a neighbor's hedge. We placed them on a rickety wood frame which we hammered together and set on our deck. A *sukkah* must have at least three walls; the outside walls of the house can be used as the fourth. It can be set on a deck or in a backyard. Whatever material is used should be strong enough to withstand normal winds. The first year we used colorful sheets as walls.

Now the entire neighborhood joins us for our *sukkah*-raising. The booth is made in our backyard of wood beams that brace it to withstand the wind. The bamboo poles still form the roof. Cornstalks, tied down with garbage-bag twists, are the walls and see-through ceiling. A staple gun helps attach the New Year's cards, paper rings, and children's pictures. The children from regular and religious school help decorate the *sukkah,* stringing popcorn, string beans, cranberries, and any leftover foods from our almost-dormant garden. Sufganiyot and cider are served to the builders. Occasionally we eat meals in our *sukkah.* Observant Jews eat all their meals there. Some Jews even sleep in their *sukkah.*

The following blessing is said when you enter and sit down in the *sukkah:*

Baruch atah Adonai Eloheinu melech ha-olam asher kidshanu b'mitzvotav ve-tzivanu leishev ba-sukkah.
Blessed art Thou, O Lord our God, King of the universe, who hast sanctified us with Thy commandments and commanded us to dwell in the sukkah.

The lulav (literally, palm branch) and the etrog (the fragrant yellow fruit of the citron) are also symbols of Sukkot. The lulav is a bouquet or small holder made with branches of willow, strands of green myrtle, and slender leaves of palm, bound together. To keep the lulav fresh throughout the holiday, it is taken apart and the branches stored in wet newspaper in the refrigerator. It is reassembled each morning. Be sure to save the lulav for Passover, when it can be used in place of the feather to search for *hametz* (see page 116). The etrog is kept in a special box or container, protected so that the tip of the fruit will not come off. After the holiday, you can put cloves in the etrog, just as you did when you "embalmed" an apple (see page 49), and use it for Havdalah the rest of the year.

When you hold the lulav and the etrog, pointing slowly in all four directions and up and down to show that God is everywhere, as are His blessings, the following prayer is said:

Baruch atah Adonai Eloheinu melech ha-olam asher kidshanu b'mitzvotav ve-tzivanu al netilat lulav.
Blessed art Thou, O Lord our God, King of the universe, who hast sanctified us with Thy commandments and commanded us about the waving of the lulav.

Since Sukkot often falls during the harvest of our backyard garden, we try to make lots of stuffed vegetable and fruit dishes. If we are lucky, we even have fresh raspberries which we pop right into our mouths from the bush.

SUKKOT STUFFED VEGETABLES

Stuffed vegetables are traditional for the harvest festival of Sukkot. They symbolize the fullness of the year to come. Sephardic Jews tend to make many dishes with stuffed vegetables. In Jerusalem, there is a tiny restaurant that serves—all year long—stuffed zucchini, eggplant, figs, carrots, green peppers, potatoes, onions, Jerusalem artichokes, tomatoes, and prunes. Let your imagination and taste help you with this recipe.

INGREDIENTS

6 medium vegetables to the
    children's liking: zucchini,
    yellow squash, green peppers,
    tomatoes, onions, large carrots,
    etc.
1 cup uncooked rice
1 teaspoon salt
2 cups boiling water
1 onion (optional)
2 tablespoons oil
1 cup frozen corn
1 cup frozen peas and carrots
2 tablespoons currants or raisins
Freshly ground pepper to taste
¼ teaspoon ground nutmeg
¼ teaspoon ground cinnamon
2 teaspoons fresh or 1 teaspoon
    dried mint
2 tablespoons chopped fresh
    parsley
1 cup stewed tomatoes

EQUIPMENT

Measuring cups
Measuring spoons
Apple corer
1½-quart pot with lid
Knife
Frying pan
4 small bowls
Spoon
Toothpicks
Large heat-resistant casserole with
    cover

SERVES
6

Child: Wash the vegetables well. Take an apple corer and tunnel out holes big enough to put in your filling. Be sure not to cut through the bottom. (See the picture on page 40.)

Child: Put the rice and the salt in the boiling water. Cover, lower the heat, and simmer for 20 minutes. Don't open the pot or the rice won't cook right.

Child with Adult: Chop the onion very well and sauté it in the oil, unless you think onions are yucky. But you would be surprised how many things taste really good with onions in them.

Child with Adult: Place the corn in one bowl, the peas and carrots in another, the rice in a third, and the currants, spices, and herbs in a fourth.

Child: Stuff whatever fillings each person particularly likes into the vegetables, leaving a slight amount of space for expansion at the top. Mark each person's vegetable with toothpicks, either different-colored ones or different numbers of toothpicks.

Child: Place the vegetables in a casserole large enough to hold them all.

Adult: Cover with the tomatoes and water to cover. Simmer, covered, for 30 minutes, or until the squash shows only the slightest resistance when pierced with the point of a sharp knife.

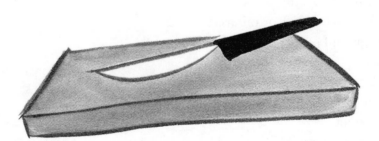

GOLDEN HARVEST TSIMMES

One of the first Yiddish words I ever learned was *tsimmes*. "Don't make a *tsimmes* out of that!" scolded my grandmother. She meant not to make a big deal out of a small thing. A tsimmes is literally a mixture of vegetables and fruit and sometimes meat, a "big deal" casserole. Whatever the other ingredients (sometimes pineapple, prunes, even puréed mango in Mexico), there is one constant ingredient—carrots.

INGREDIENTS

4 carrots
2 sweet potatoes or yams
1½ pounds Hubbard squash
3 quarts salted water
2 apples
¼ cup raisins
½ cup orange juice
¼ cup brown sugar
1 teaspoon ground cinnamon
4 tablespoons (½ stick) margarine
    or butter

EQUIPMENT

Measuring cups
Measuring spoons
Paring knife or vegetable peeler
Plastic knife
Pot with lid
Apple corer
Ovenproof casserole or foil baking
    cups

SERVES
8

Adult: Use your imagination on this one. Make it with dates, prunes, pumpkins—whatever foods your children like.

Child: Peel the carrots, sweet potatoes or yams, and squash. Using a plastic knife, cut them in half or, if large, in quarters.

Adult: Boil the carrots, sweet potatoes or yams, and squash in salted water, covered, for 10 minutes, or until tender. Cool and peel. Cut the vegetables in circles or any shape the children want.

Child: Core the apples. Slice them in circles.

Adult: Preheat oven to 400°.

Child: Grease an oblong or circular casserole and decorate the bottom with the vegetables and then the apples. Or make your own individual tsimmes in foil baking cups. When David was four, he created a face: the head was slices of sweet potatoes, the eyes were carrots, the nose was an apple, and the mouth a slice of Hubbard squash. Sprinkle with the raisins. Pour the orange juice over it. Sprinkle with brown sugar and cinnamon, and dot with margarine or butter.

Adult: Bake for 25 minutes, or until well browned.

ZUCCHINI BREAD

This variation on the late James Beard's recipe has been a staple ever since I picked the first zucchini from our garden.

INGREDIENTS

3 eggs
1½ cups sugar
1 cup vegetable oil
3 teaspoons vanilla extract
2 cups unpeeled raw zucchini
3 cups all-purpose flour
1 teaspoon salt
1 teaspoon baking soda
¼ teaspoon double-acting baking powder
3 teaspoons ground cinnamon
½ teaspoon ground nutmeg
1 cup coarsely chopped walnuts, raisins, or coconut

EQUIPMENT

Measuring cups
Measuring spoons
Mixing bowl or electric mixer
Fork or wire whisk
Grater or food processor
Spoon
2 greased 9 by 5-inch loaf pans
Rubber scraper
Cooling rack

MAKES
2 LOAVES

Child: Beat the eggs until light and foamy. Add the sugar, oil, and vanilla, and mix gently but well.

Adult with Child: Grate the zucchini by hand or show the child how to use the steel blade of a food processor. Add to the egg mixture.

Adult: Preheat oven to 350°.

Child: Mix together the flour, salt, baking soda, baking powder, cinnamon, and nutmeg. Add to the zucchini mixture. Stir until well blended. Add the nuts and pour into the loaf pans, getting out any leftover batter with a rubber scraper. Fingers are allowed for licking.

Adult: Bake for 1 hour. Cool on a rack.

KIDS' QUICHE WITH VEGGIES

This is a great main dish for leftover vegetables and cheese. If my children help make this dish, then they will be more likely to eat it. Once you've figured out the main formula for making quiche, the rest is easy. You can do this with all kinds of vegetables. I have made this with broccoli and spinach. Buy a frozen prepared crust or make your own, which is much easier to do than many people realize and great fun. Also, this dish makes good use of leftover cheese in your refrigerator.

INGREDIENTS

CRUST:

1 9-inch prepared crust

or

4 tablespoons (½ stick) unsalted
butter or margarine

4 tablespoons Crisco

1¼ cups all-purpose flour

Pinch of salt

2 tablespoons cold water

FILLING:

3 large eggs

2 cups milk

Salt and freshly ground pepper to
taste

Ground nutmeg to taste

½ cup sharp hard cheese like
cheddar or Gruyère

3 cups broccoli

EQUIPMENT

Food processor

Measuring cups

Measuring spoons

Plastic wrap

Rolling pin

9-inch deep dish pie pan

Mixing bowl

Fork or wire whisk

Mixing spoon

MAKES
1 QUICHE

To make your own crust:

Adult with Child: Using a food processor, combine the butter or margarine, Crisco, flour, and salt. Spin or blend well until crumbly, slowly adding the cold water. When a soft ball forms, wrap it in plastic wrap and refrigerate for about 1 hour, or until firm.

Adult: Preheat oven to 400°.

Adult with Child: On a lightly floured surface, roll dough into a circle about ⅛ inch thick. Don't bear down on the rolling pin. Just move it from the center away from you easily. It will flatten more gently that way. When dough is ⅛ inch thick, lay it in the bottom and up the sides of a 9-inch deep dish pie pan, shaping it to fit the pan. Pinch the edges to trim any extra dough. Prick the bottom of the dough a few times with the tines of a fork and bake for 10 minutes, or until golden brown.

To make the filling:

Child: In a mixing bowl, beat the eggs well. Add the milk, salt, pepper, nutmeg, and the cheese. Mix well. Add the broccoli and mix well again.

Adult with Child: Carefully pour the mixture into the pie pan lined with either your homemade crust or the prepared one. Lower the heat to 375° and bake for 30 minutes, or until set. Slice and serve with a salad.

PASTA WITH VEGETABLES AND PINE NUTS

This pasta dish with a kind of pesto sauce is a favorite of my children. I think it is particularly appropriate during Sukkot when green beans are still being harvested in our garden and the weather is still warm. Snipping beans is a great occupation, even in front of the television. You can add or substitute zucchini, yellow squash, eggplant, or any other vegetable in your garden or supermarket. Let the children decide which vegetables and which pasta. Try to mix shapes or colors. Just remember that rigatoni expands more than tubular shapes, so measure accordingly. If using linguine in combination with shell shapes, break the linguine strands before cooking.

INGREDIENTS

¼ cup virgin olive oil

2 cups packed fresh basil leaves

Salt to taste

4 cups fresh green beans or other vegetables

½ pound pasta in different shapes and colors

4 tablespoons pine nuts

2 tablespoons unsalted butter or vegetable oil

2 cloves garlic, minced

¾ cup freshly grated imported Parmesan cheese

Freshly grated pepper to taste

12 cherry tomatoes

EQUIPMENT

Food processor

2 large pots with lids

Medium pot

Knife

Colander or strainer

Serving bowl

Sukkot

SERVES 4–6

Adult with Child: Put the olive oil and basil leaves in a food processor and use the on-off motion to combine but not pulverize. Set aside.

Adult: Fill two large pots with cold water and a little salt. Cover and bring to a boil.

Child: Put the green beans in the colander or strainer and wash under cold water. Then find a comfortable spot to sit or stand and carefully break off both pointed ends of each green bean. Set aside the beans.

Adult with Child: Here is a math problem. Figure out how long it takes to cook the pasta and the green beans. Then put the pasta in one pot and cook according to the directions on the package. Place the green beans in the other and cook between 10 and 15 minutes and then plunge into iced water to retain the color.

Child: While the pasta and vegetables are cooking, toast the pine nuts in a toaster oven at 350° for about 5 minutes.

Adult with Child: Place the butter in a large pasta bowl. Add the pine nuts and the garlic and then toss with the drained pasta and the green beans. Add the basil-oil mixture and then the cheeses. Adjust to taste, adding more cheese, basil, or oil as needed. Mix with freshly grated pepper and garnish with cherry tomatoes. Serve lukewarm or at room temperature.

HANUKKAH

HANUKKAH LATKE PARTY MENU

Edible Menorahs*
Potato-Vegetable Latkes*
Applesauce*
Aunt Lisl's Butter Cookies*
Edible Dreidels*

HANUKKAH SHABBAT DINNER

Matzah Ball Soup*
Friday Night Pot Roast*
Potato-Vegetable Latkes*
Applesauce*
Sufganiyot*

HANUKKAH DREIDEL BIRTHDAY PARTY

To make and to eat at the party:

Pretzel Bagels*
Hanukkah Dreidel Sandwiches*
Gingerbread Dreidels*
Edible Dreidels*
Candle Cupcakes*

HANUKKAH

"Can you guess, children, which is the best of all holidays? Hanukkah, of course. . . . You eat pancakes every day," said Sholem Aleichem. And who doesn't like potato latkes? These Russian potato pancakes were once a poor man's dish cooked in goose fat, symbolizing the oil that burned for eight days.

Although Hanukkah, the Festival of Lights, is a relatively minor religious holiday, it has assumed major importance in our country, coming right at Christmas time. In our family, we do not try to compete with Christmas. I explain that everyone has a winter holiday to brighten up those cold days and then, of course, we go into the traditions of Hanukkah.

My husband tells the story of the weak conquering the mighty over two thousand years ago, when the Maccabee brothers defeated the Syrian King Antiochus' huge army, which was trying to make the Jews give up their religion. When the Temple was clean, the people wanted to light the menorah. There was only enough oil for one day, but by a miracle it burned for eight days. And so we celebrate Hanukkah to commemorate the rededication of the Temple in Jerusalem.

In our house, we celebrate with our very close friends and their children. It is a joyful, fun-filled time, with presents for each child, dreidel spinning, and a festive meal of pot roast, potato pancakes, applesauce, and Hanukkah cookies which the children help prepare.

EDIBLE DREIDEL

O dreidel, dreidel, dreidel
I made it out of clay
And when it's dry and ready
Then dreidel I shall play.

My favorite Hanukkah song. While eating sufganiyot (Israeli jelly dough-nuts) and potato latkes, what better thing to do than play dreidel, once a German gambling game? The rules are simple. The letters written on the four-sided top are *nun*, נ (nothing), *gimel,* ג (all), *heh,* ה (half), and *shin,* ש (add two things to the pot). Together, the letters mean "a great miracle happened here." Each person should start with about ten pennies, carob chips, nuts, raisins, M&M's, or stones. Each player puts one in the pot. In turn, each person spins the dreidel, which is like a top. The face-up letter determines what he wins. When the pot is empty, each player adds one object to it. If an odd number of objects are in the pot, the *heh* person takes half plus one. When one person wins everything, the game is over.

When the children have tired of playing dreidel, they can make an edible one.

INGREDIENTS
1 marshmallow
1 toothpick
1 Hershey's kiss

MAKES
1

Child: Thread the toothpick through the marshmallow. Add the kiss to the end. Eat it, don't spin it!

EDIBLE MENORAH

The menorah is the most meaningful symbol of Hanukkah. Artistic Jews throughout the world have created their own versions. I like to take our children to local Jewish gift shops, synagogues, and museums to see the different renditions. One Hanukkah we spent in Jerusalem delighting in menorahs in windows.

Lighting the menorah is always confusing. For each of the eight nights of Hanukkah, an additional candle is inserted, from right to left, and lit by the *shammas,* or helper candle, from left to right, until the eight-candled menorah is aglow. We place our menorahs on a flame-proof tray in our front window. If your children do not want to make their own menorah out of clay, let them make the following edible one.

INGREDIENTS

1 slice white bread
Peanut butter
9 carrot rounds
9 pretzel sticks
9 raisins

EQUIPMENT

Plate
Knife

MAKES
1

Child: Place the bread on the plate. Press down to flatten it (don't cut off the crust). Spread it with the peanut butter. Stick the carrots onto the peanut butter as bases for the candles, placing one higher or lower for the *shammas.* Stick the pretzels flat on the peanut butter to be the candles, and use raisins for the flames.

The result is a flat picture—the pretzels do not stick up from the bread.

POTATO-VEGETABLE LATKES

This is a colorful variation on the classic potato latke.

INGREDIENTS

2 large potatoes
2 large carrots
2 medium-size zucchini
1 large onion
3 eggs, beaten
½ teaspoon salt
⅛ teaspoon pepper
¾ cup matzah meal
Vegetable oil for frying

EQUIPMENT

Vegetable peeler
Measuring cups
Measuring spoons
Food processor or hand grater
Mixing bowl
Spoon
10-inch frying pan
Pancake turner
Paper towels
Baking sheet (optional)

MAKES 24–36, DEPENDING ON SIZE

Child: Peel the potatoes and the carrots. Put the potatoes in cold water.

Adult with Child: This is a perfect way to teach your child how to use the food processor. Depending on the age, keep a good watch over him or her. Use the steel blade or the shredding blade to grate the zucchini, potatoes, carrots, and onion. Show the child how to use the "pulse" button or turn the machine on and off frequently so the vegetables don't turn into the soupy mess called a purée. Vegetables can also be grated by hand with an aluminum grater.

Child: In a bowl, mix together the grated vegetables, beaten eggs, salt, and pepper. Stir in the matzah meal. Shape the batter into pancakes, using 1–2 tablespoons of mixture for each.

Adult with Child: Fry the latkes, a few at a time, in 1–2 tablespoons hot oil for 1½ minutes per side. Add additional oil as necessary. Drain on paper towels. Serve hot with applesauce.

Note: If desired, fry the latkes ahead of time and drain on paper towels for 1–2 hours at room temperature. Reheat on an ungreased baking sheet in a 350° oven for 8–10 minutes. You can also freeze the latkes and store them. Reheat in a 350° oven for about 15 minutes.

APPLESAUCE

This is a recipe with which our children love to improvise.

INGREDIENTS
4 pounds very red baking apples
1 lemon
Handful of Red Hots for color, and to taste
½ cup apple juice, cider, or water
Honey or maple syrup, to taste

EQUIPMENT
Measuring cup
Knife
Heavy pot with lid
Wooden spoon
Food mill
Mixing bowl

MAKES 4 CUPS

Child: Cut the apples and lemon into quarters. Place in a heavy pot with the Red Hots. Add the apple juice, cider, or water.

Adult: Cover the pot, bring to a boil, and then simmer over low heat, stirring occasionally to turn the apples and make sure they do not stick. You may want to add some more liquid. Cook about 20 minutes, or until the apples are soft. Let cool slightly.

Child with Adult: Put the sauce through a food mill and adjust the flavor by adding honey or maple syrup to taste. Refrigerate until ready to serve.

GINGERBREAD DREIDELS

Although my family does not celebrate Christmas, there is one thing that I have always wanted to make and that is a gingerbread house. We came up instead with the idea of making gingerbread dreidels cut out from a pattern (which follows here) or with a Hanukkah dreidel cookie cutter. German Jews enjoyed gingerbread in the wintertime, and these cookies taste good whether constructed into a three-dimensional dreidel or just cut out, decorated, and served individually. The 3-D dreidel is a great activity for busy people because it has to be made in stages.

INGREDIENTS

COOKIES:

½ cup dark brown sugar

1½ cups (3 sticks) unsalted butter or *pareve* margarine

½ cup molasses

3 teaspoons ground cinnamon

3 teaspoons ground ginger

2 teaspoons ground cloves

1 cup plus 1 teaspoon water

½ tablespoon baking soda

5 cups all-purpose flour (about)

ICING:

3–3½ cups sifted confectioners' sugar

3 egg whites

1 teaspoon lemon juice

Blue food coloring

EQUIPMENT

Food processor

Electric beater

Mixing bowl

Plastic spatula

Metal spatula

Small knife

Baking sheets

Rolling pin

Cooling rack

Bowls

8 by 8-inch baking dish

Rectangular baking pan

Small spatula

Cardboard

Scissors

Paper-towel center tube

Pastry tube

Candies for decorating

MAKES ABOUT 50 INDIVIDUAL DREIDEL COOKIES OR 1 3-D DREIDEL WITH LEFTOVER DOUGH FOR SOME COOKIES

Adult: Using the steel blade of a food processor, cream the sugar and butter or margarine until they are very well blended. It is important to blend well.

Child with Adult: Add the molasses and spices and blend well again. Using a plastic spatula, fold 1 cup of the water into the butter-molasses mixture. Dilute the baking soda in the remaining teaspoon of water and blend it well into the batter. Still using the food processor, work in the flour until the dough is fairly stiff.

Child: Remove the dough to a mixing bowl and smooth it into a round ball. Cover the dough and let it stand overnight in a refrigerator or cool place.

Child: If you are making the 3-D dreidel, trace the dreidel rectangle, triangle, square, and template below onto cardboard. Cut out the patterns.

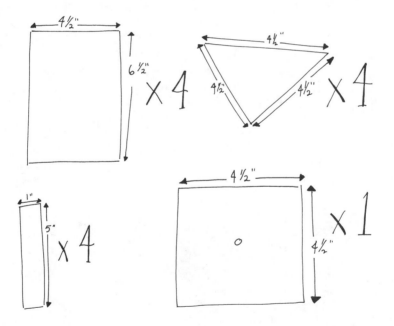

Adult: When you are ready to cut out the cookies, let the dough stand at room temperature about ½ hour before starting. Preheat oven to 350°. Grease 2 baking sheets.

blend butter & sugar

add molasses & spices

add flour & baking soda

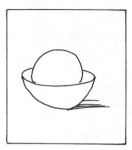

form dough into ball

make dreidel patterns

roll out dough

cut out dreidel pieces

bake dreidel pieces

mix sugar, egg whites, lemon juice

beat till smooth

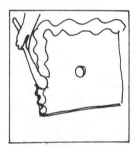

color one third blue

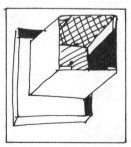

apply icing to square

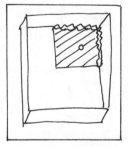

place square in pan corner

attach two rectangles, template along seam

attach remaining rectangles, templates

Child with Adult: Flour a board and rolling pin lightly and roll out a small piece of dough to test if it is the right consistency. If it is not stiff enough, work in more flour. Roll the dough until flat and thin, about ⅛ inch, and cut out the cookies with a Hanukkah dreidel cookie cutter. If making the 3-D dreidel, use the cardboard patterns to cut out the pieces. Be sure to put a small hole, big enough to insert a candy cane, in the square, which will be the top. You will need to make 3 more copies of the rectangle, triangle, and template. Place the cookies or dreidel pieces about 4 inches apart on the baking sheet and bake for 5–7 minutes, or until they are nicely browned. Using a metal spatula, carefully remove each cookie to a drying rack. For the 3-D dreidel, it is better to overcook than undercook.

Adult: To prepare the icing, place the confectioners' sugar in a bowl and add the egg whites and lemon juice and beat until the mixture is very smooth. The consistency should be quite stiff, as this icing becomes the "glue" that holds together the 3-D dreidel. Take a third of the icing and transfer it to a different bowl. Add blue food coloring to that.

Adult with Child: Take the square with the hole in the center and, using a small spatula or a knife, put some icing evenly along 2 adjacent sides. Place the square in the corner of a rectangular baking pan, so that you can use the high sides of the pan as supports for the walls of your dreidel. Attach 2 gingerbread rectangles to the square base at right angles and use icing to stick the adjacent edges together. Add the template stick vertically on the inside with more icing to support the seam where the rectangles are joined.

Now you have half of a box! Gently turn it around to face the corner of the pan to build the other 2 walls, attaching the two remaining gingerbread rectangles first to the square base, and then to each other, and finally supporting each corner with a vertical template. When you are finished, the 4-sided body of the dreidel will stand together on its own. Let the icing dry until the pieces are firmly "glued" together. Leave it this way overnight if you want. Put the leftover icing in a bowl and carefully cover with plastic wrap. Refrigerate overnight. If it is too stiff, add a drop or two of lemon juice or water.

The next day, use the blue icing in a pastry tube to write a different Hebrew letter on each of the 4 rectangular sides of the dreidel: *nun* (נ), *gimel* (ג), *heh* (ה), *shin* (ש). Make sure the dreidel is right-side up before you begin—that is, the square base with the hole in it should be on top, or your letters will be upside down.

write Hebrew letters

put cardboard roll
in dreidel

form point with
triangles

insert candy cane

When you finish the letters, set the dreidel box back on its square base; you are ready to assemble the pointed tip. Cut the cardboard paper-towel roll to stand a little taller than the dreidel walls and place it inside the box. You want it to be a ballast for the triangles. Paint icing along the sides of the triangles and set them in place adjoining the box. Let them dry for a few hours. Then carefully pick up the dreidel and rest it on its side. Insert a candy cane, lollipop, chocolate peppermint stick, or even a plastic spoon handle into the hole. Decorate with icing, using more icing to glue on candies and raisins, and use your dreidel as the centerpiece for your Hanukkah party. Make sure you eat it afterwards!

CANDLE CUPCAKES

Making your own menorah is one of the great pleasures of celebrating Hanukkah. Menorahs can come in all different shapes, made from nearly any materials, as long as each candle is kept separate and distinct from the others and they are in one line with the *shammas* raised. These candle cupcakes can be arranged together in nearly any shape—a circle, square, straight line, or whatever you can imagine—to form a different and deliciously edible menorah.

INGREDIENTS

14 cream-filled chocolate sandwich cookies
3 tablespoons unsalted butter
1 pint chocolate ice cream or
  frozen yoghurt
Fresh raspberries for garnish

EQUIPMENT

Food processor
Saucepan
Muffin tins
Paper cupcake liners
Large spoon
Hanukkah candles

MAKES AT LEAST 12 CUP-
CAKES, 9 TO MAKE
YOUR MENORAH
AND A FEW EXTRA
TO ENJOY RIGHT
AWAY

Adult: To make the crust, whirl 12 of the cookies in a food processor until ground very fine. Melt the butter in a small saucepan or microwave and mix well with the cookies.

Child: Put one paper cupcake liner in each muffin mold. Using your fingers, press some of the cookie-butter mixture along the bottom and up the sides of each mold. Try to get the cookie mixture pressed together as smoothly and evenly as you can. Remove the ice cream or frozen yoghurt from the freezer and let it soften slightly for a few minutes, then spoon it into the cookie molds, pressing down until smooth. Fill the molds with the ice cream or frozen yoghurt.

Adult: Place the filled tins in the freezer until they hold together well, about 3 hours or until you're ready to use them.

Child: Insert a Hanukkah candle into the center of each cupcake. Refreeze until very solid in the tins, and wrap well. (You can even do this a week ahead.) When ready to make your menorah, remove the tins from the freezer, then carefully remove each cupcake, with its liner, from the tins. Arrange the menorah as you wish—in a row or a circle, but make sure to elevate the *shammas* by placing it on the remaining two sandwich cookies. Then immediately light the candles and say the blessings. Of course, this doesn't take the place of the real menorah. Be sure to blow out the candles before the ice cream gets soft!

HANUKKAH DREIDEL SANDWICHES

Use Hanukkah cookie cutters or scissors to make your own dreidel sandwiches. If you want them to be Israeli, make them out of pita bread and substitute hummus (see page 105) for peanut butter.

INGREDIENTS
2 pieces loaf bread
    or 1 pita bread
Peanut butter
Hummus
Honey
Raisins
Banana

EQUIPMENT
Cookie cutters
Plastic knife

MAKES
AT LEAST 1
SANDWICH

Child: For this one you can be as creative as you wish. Take the bread and the cookie cutters and cut out shapes. Make sure that you do 2 of each shape. Spread your preferred filling on one of each shape of the bread. Add raisins and/or banana. Put a matching bread shape on top of the filling and eat.

HOMEMADE PEANUT BUTTER

INGREDIENTS
1 cup peanuts
1 tablespoon vegetable oil
1 teaspoon salt
Sugar to taste

EQUIPMENT
Food processor or mortar and
   pestle
Spoon

MAKES ABOUT 1 CUP

Adult with Child: Place the peanuts and the oil in either the food processor . . . or a mortar and pestle, depending on how much energy you want your children to expend. Blend or pound until pulverized, stopping at chunky or smooth peanut butter. Add salt or sugar to taste and additional vegetable oil if you want it creamier.

AUNT LISL'S BUTTER COOKIES

When I was a little girl, my aunt Lisl always made butter cookies at Hanukkah time. We decorated them. The cookies were stored in her garage in airtight containers. Sometimes we got to take some of them home. Other times, we just nibbled on them at her house.

One of the best things about cooking with relatives is that it's a great time to ask for family stories. While we baked, Aunt Lisl told wonderful tales of my father's boyhood in Germany.

INGREDIENTS

½ pound (2 sticks) unsalted butter
   or margarine, softened
¾ cup sugar
2 eggs
1 tablespoon brandy (optional)
Dash of salt
½ teaspoon vanilla
3½ cups flour
1 egg yolk
Chopped nuts and raisins
   or
1 egg white
Coarse sugar colored with blue
   food coloring

EQUIPMENT

Measuring cup
Measuring spoons
Mixing bowl
Wooden spoon
Cookie cutters or toothpicks
Rolling pin
Greased baking sheet
Pastry brush
Metal spatula
Cooling rack

MAKES
ABOUT
48

Child: In a bowl, cream the butter and sugar. Then mix in the eggs, brandy, salt, vanilla, and flour. Let rest for at least 30 minutes in the refrigerator.

Adult with Child: Roll out the dough to ⅛ inch thick. Preheat oven to 350°.

Child: You can either use cookie cutters or use the point of a toothpick like a knife to cut out cookies in any shapes you want. Let your imagination run free: how about dreidels, Stars of David, candles with flames attached, the four Hebrew letters on the dreidel?

Once you have cut out the cookies, gently place them on the baking sheet. Then either brush them with egg yolk and sprinkle with nuts and raisins or brush with egg white and sprinkle with blue sugar.

Adult: Bake for about 10 minutes, or until golden brown. Use a metal spatula to gently remove each cookie from the baking sheet to a cooling rack or flat plate.

DANIELA'S BROWNIES

My children like to visit my aunt Lisl's daughter-in-law Dorothy the way I used to visit Aunt Lisl.

Dorothy doesn't make butter cookies, but she does make brownies, which she serves at Hanukkah and every Friday night, a perfect ending to a meat meal. The children help make the brownies and then take a few extra home in aluminum foil. They love them—without the nuts.

INGREDIENTS

⅔ cup unsifted flour
¼ teaspoon salt
½ teaspoon baking powder
2 eggs
1 cup sugar
⅓ cup (⅔ stick) *pareve* margarine
2 ounces (2 squares) unsweetened chocolate, melted
1 teaspoon vanilla
½ cup chopped nuts (optional)
Confectioners' sugar

EQUIPMENT

Measuring cups
Measuring spoons
Mixing bowls
Wooden spoon
Fork or wire whisk
Greased 8-inch square pan
Rubber scraper
Spatula

MAKES ABOUT 18

Child: Mix together the flour, salt, and baking powder. Set aside. Beat the eggs well. Gradually beat the sugar into the eggs, then beat in the margarine and chocolate. Mix in the flour mixture. Stir in the vanilla and nuts, and place in the baking pan.

Adult: Preheat oven to 350°.

Child: Bake for 25 minutes. Let cool, then dust with confectioners' sugar and cut into squares.

SUFGANIYOT

The young State of Israel has created many of its own customs. One is serving jelly doughnuts at Hanukkah, which are fried in oil to symbolize the miracle of the oil that lasted for eight days instead of one.

INGREDIENTS

1 scant tablespoon (1 package) dry yeast
4 tablespoons sugar
¾ cup lukewarm milk or warm water*
2½ cups all-purpose flour
Pinch of salt
1 teaspoon ground cinnamon
2 eggs, separated
2 tablespoons (¼ stick) butter or *pareve* margarine, softened*
Apricot or strawberry preserves
Vegetable oil for deep-frying
Sugar

EQUIPMENT

Measuring spoons
Measuring cups
Mixing bowls
Spoon
Sifter
Clean dish towel
Rolling pin
Juice glass
Deep fryer or heavy pot
Slotted spoon
Paper towels
Tiny spoon

MAKES ABOUT 12

* Use butter and milk if serving at a milk meal, and water and *pareve* margarine for a meat meal.

Child: Mix together the yeast, 2 tablespoons of the sugar, and the milk. Let sit to make sure it bubbles.

Child: Sift the flour and mix it with the remaining sugar, salt, cinnamon, egg yolks, and the yeast mixture.

Adult with Child: Knead the dough until it forms a ball. Add the butter or margarine. Knead some more, until the butter is well absorbed. Cover with a towel and let rise overnight in the refrigerator.

Adult: Roll out the dough to a thickness of ⅛ inch.

Child: Cut out the dough into 24 rounds with a juice glass, or any object about 2 inches in diameter. Take ½ teaspoon of preserves and place in center of 12 rounds. Top with the other 12. Press down at edges, sealing with egg whites. Crimping with the thumb and second finger is best. Let rise for about 30 minutes.

Adult: Heat 2 inches of oil to about 375°. Drop the doughnuts into the hot oil, about 5 at a time. Turn to brown on both sides. Drain on paper towels.

Child: Roll the doughnuts in sugar.

TU B'SHEVAT

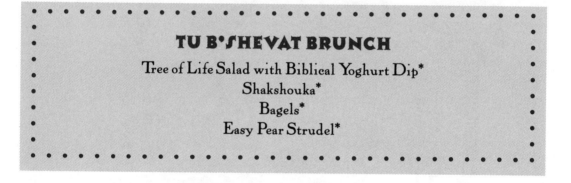

TU B'SHEVAT DINNER

Tu B'Shevat Hallah*
Fruitful Salad*
Golden Harvest Tsimmes*
Stuffed Figs and Dates*

TU B'SHEVAT BRUNCH

Tree of Life Salad with Biblical Yoghurt Dip*
Shakshouka*
Bagels*
Easy Pear Strudel*

TU B'SHEVAT

Ever since I was a child I have confused Tu B'Shevat and Tisha B'Av. To this day, I do a quick mental month calculation after each one is mentioned. Tu B'Shevat, the holiday that heralds the start of spring in Israel with the first almond blossoms, falls in January or February. Tisha B'Av, the holy day on which we mourn the destruction of the Temple, comes in the heat of July or August.

My strongest childhood memories of Tu B'Shevat are of the blue-and-white Jewish National Fund boxes into which I dutifully plunked my nickels and dimes to "plant trees in Israel." But not until I went to live in Jerusalem did I understand the real significance of the holiday, which is observed on the 15th day of the Hebrew month of Shevat. During this month of heavy rains that mark the end of winter and the beginning of spring, the sap in the fruit trees begins to rise. It is the Arbor Day of Israel. If it is not the right season for planting in your part of the country, start seedlings of parsley, lima beans, or sweet potatoes inside at Tu B'Shevat. The parsley will be ready to use on the Seder plate at Passover.

I had hardly learned my *alef-bet* at Ulpan Etzion in Jerusalem when I attended my first Tu B'Shevat tree-planting party in Caesarea. The food was not fancy, but nuts and fruits abounded, to celebrate the "New Year of the Trees." It is customary to eat up to fifteen different kinds of fruits and nuts such as carob, plums, pomegranates, pears, citrons, oranges, apples, dates, grapes, nuts, melons, and apricots. Carob pods (or carob chips made from the pods) are traditionally chewed in Israel at Tu B'Shevat—they taste like chocolate!

While the guests were munching on dried fruits and nuts, all the time basking in the winter sunshine near the sea, they played a game. Someone would name a fruit or nut, and we would try to find a biblical passage mentioning its name. Others discussed the symbolic meanings of the fruits and nuts. Here are a few:

Apple—symbol of a sweet year. But there are no apples in the Bible, not even in the Garden of Eden!

Apricot—glowing splendor of God. Apples in the Bible stand for quinces or apricots, either one possibly the "apple" of Adam and Eve.

Almond—blossoms of the almond, the first tree to bloom, stand for the swiftness of divine judgment.

Carob—the food of the poor, represents humility, and it tastes like chocolate.

Pomegranate—because of its many seeds and bright red color, a symbol of fertility, peace, and prosperity.

My children's Hebrew school holds a Tu B'Shevat Seder, a Sephardic custom started in Spain and Middle Eastern countries. The children drink four cups of "wine" which symbolize the changes that nature undergoes in the four seasons. The lightest, apple juice, stands for the slumber that descends upon nature in the fall.

Then, to symbolize the changes, the children drink orange, then cranberry, and finally dark grape juice, which evokes the awakening and blossoming of nature on Shevat 15.

At the Seder meal the children taste pieces of three different categories of fruits and nuts. They first pick up a new fruit of the season and then taste from five to fifteen different fruits. The first category of fruit has a peel or a shell that cannot be eaten: pistachio nuts, bananas, kiwis, oranges, avocados, almonds, pineapples, melons, etc. The second has a pit inside that cannot be eaten: prunes, dates, apricots, plums, cherries, olives, etc. The third fruit can be eaten entirely: strawberries, seedless grapes, pears, figs, apples, and raisins. Before the fruit is eaten the following blessing is recited:

**Baruch atah Adonai Eloheinu melech ha-olam,
borei p'ri ha-etz.
Blessed art Thou, O Lord our God, King of the universe,
who createst the fruit of the tree.**

At our home we try to have a fruit and nut meal at Tu B'Shevat. You can even add nuts and raisins to your hallah.

TU B'SHEVAT HALLAH

Follow the recipe on pages 7–9 for hallah. Just before the first rising, fold into the dough a cup of mixed chopped walnuts, dates, and raisins.

FRUITFUL SALAD

INGREDIENTS

1 orange, peeled, cut into round
   slices
1 avocado, sliced
1 apple, peeled and diced
2 pitted dates, diced small
Seeds of ¼ pomegranate or ¼
   cup dried or fresh cranberries
¼ cup roasted pecans
½ head romaine lettuce
4 tablespoons mayonnaise

EQUIPMENT

Measuring cup
Measuring spoon
Salad bowl
Salad spoons

SERVES 6

Child: Combine the fruits and lettuce in a salad bowl. Just before serving, mix in the mayonnaise. Toss 15 times in honor of the 15 different kinds of fruits and nuts eaten on Shevat 15.

FRUIT KUGEL

In Eastern Europe, a kugel was the Sabbath dessert, a sweet noodle or potato dish often made with fruit. I can cajole my children into eating dishes they don't want—as long as they know a kugel is coming afterward.

INGREDIENTS

8 ounces broad noodles

Vegetable oil

4 tablespoons (½ stick) butter or
    margarine

3 eggs

½ cup sugar

½ pound pot cheese

1 cup sour cream

1 cup milk

1 teaspoon vanilla

1 teaspoon ground cinnamon

½ 8-ounce can crushed pineapple
    with juice

1 apple, diced

1 pear, diced

1 orange, peeled and diced

¼ cup dried apricots

¼ cup pitted prunes

Pineapple rings

Maraschino cherries

EQUIPMENT

Measuring spoons

Measuring cups

Large pot

Colander

Small saucepan

Mixing bowls

Fork or wire whisk

Wooden spoon

9 by 13-inch baking dish

Rubber scraper

SERVES
8

Adult: Partially cook the noodles in salted water with 1 teaspoon oil according to the directions on the label (the oil helps separate the strands). Rinse and drain.

Adult: In a saucepan, melt the butter or margarine. Let cool (otherwise the eggs will curdle). Combine with the eggs and beat well. Preheat oven to 350°.

Child: Mix together the noodles, egg mixture, sugar, pot cheese, sour cream, milk, flavorings, and all the fruits except the pineapple rings and cherries.

Child: Grease the baking dish with vegetable oil. Pour in the kugel. Place pineapple rings on top, with a cherry in the middle of each ring.

Adult: Bake for 40–60 minutes, or until golden.

Note: Don't let the number of ingredients scare you. This is a perfect kugel for improvisation and a way for children to add or subtract the fruits they want. Use what you want in your kugel. It will still taste delicious with a dairy meal.

TREE OF LIFE SALAD

**SERVES
6**

This is a wonderfully creative recipe with veggies that you craft into a tree of life using broccoli, cherry tomatoes or pomegranates, carrot for the trunk, slices of green pepper for the grass, and round slices of yellow pepper for the sun. Remember that Adam and Eve in the Garden of Eden were forbidden to eat from the tree of knowledge—but the tree of life you can eat! Serve with hummus (page 105) or a biblical yoghurt dip.

INGREDIENTS

1 bunch broccoli
Salt to taste
1 carrot
1 green pepper
1 yellow pepper
1 handful cherry tomatoes

EQUIPMENT

Knife
Pot with water
Slotted spoon
Vegetable peeler
Mixing bowl with ice and water
Serving platter

Adult with Child: Cut the broccoli into flowerets.

Adult: Bring a pot of water to a boil. Add a little salt and the broccoli. Let it cook for about 5 minutes. Then, using a slotted spoon, remove the broccoli and place in a mixing bowl with ice and water. (You can steam the broccoli instead if you like.)

Child: Peel the carrot.

Adult: Cut the carrot in half lengthwise, and slice the peppers. Place all the vegetables out on a platter or in individual bowls so the children can work with them easily.

Child: Using the ingredients, make the tree of life with the apple and the snake.

BIBLICAL YOGHURT DIP

With today's rediscovery of yoghurt, this is a healthful and tasty way to get your children to eat their vegetables.

INGREDIENTS
1 cucumber
1 cup yoghurt
2 cloves garlic, mashed
½ cup fresh mint
Salt to taste

EQUIPMENT
Vegetable peeler
Knife
Measuring cups
Food processor

MAKES 1 CUP

Child: Peel the cucumber and cut in half.

Adult with Child: Place the yoghurt, the garlic, the cucumber, and the mint in a food processor and pulse on and off. You do not want a puree. Add salt to taste and place the dip in the refrigerator for several hours. Drain off any liquid that accumulates.

STUFFED FIGS AND DATES

An old Jewish man in ancient Israel was planting a fig tree. The Roman Emperor passed by and said to him, "Why do you do that, old man? Surely you will not live long enough to see it bear fruit."

"In that case," replied the man, "I will leave it for my son, as my father left the fruit of his labor for me."

The Emperor admired his spirit. "If you do live to see the figs on your tree ripen," he said, "let me know about it."

The old man lived to eat of the fruit and, remembering the Emperor's words, brought him a basket of figs. The Emperor was so pleased that he filled the old man's basket with gold.

A greedy woman who heard of the gift made her husband go to the Emperor too. "He loves figs," she said, "and he will surely fill your basket with gold."

The man listened to his wife, brought the figs to the palace, and said, "These figs are for the Emperor. Empty my basket and fill it with gold!"

When the Emperor heard this, he ordered the guard to have all the people who passed by throw figs at the man. When the man finally escaped, he ran home and told his wife what had happened.

"Well," she said, "you are lucky. Think what would have happened if the figs had been coconuts!"

At the Sephardic Seder, figs stuffed with nuts and rolled in coconut are a common delicacy.

INGREDIENTS

2 cups water

12 almonds with skins

6 walnuts or pecans in the shell

12 dried figs

12 dates, pitted

Grated coconut

EQUIPMENT

Small saucepan

Small bowl

Nutcracker

Knife

White paper candy cups

MAKES
24

Adult: Bring water to a boil. Let sit for a minute. Pour over the almonds.

Child: After about 5 minutes, when the water is cool enough to handle, take each almond and rub it between your fingers until the skin slides off.

This is called blanching almonds. Be careful that your almond doesn't skid across the table.

Child: Crack open the walnuts and pecans. Carefully remove the nut meats and divide in half. Throw out the shells.

Adult with Child: Slit the center of each fig and date with a knife. Place an almond or half a walnut or pecan in the center of each fruit. Close up, and roll the stuffed fruit in grated coconut. Place in small white paper cups.

PURIM

PURIM DINNER

Hallah*

Hummus*

Orange Chicken*

Green Vegetables

Hamantashen*

SHALACH MANOT PLATE

No-Bake Marshmallow Cookies*

Hamantashen*

Apples "Embalmed" with Cloves*

Aunt Lisl's Butter Cookies*

Stuffed Figs and Dates*

Golda Meir's Chocolate-Chip Cookies*

Chocolate-Chip Kisses*

PURIM

Purim places a greater emphasis on physical delights than does any other Jewish holiday. When the feast day approaches, troubles are forgotten and festivities begin. It is a holiday of letting go, of donning costumes and participating in parades, parties, and carnivals, of preparing an elaborate meal at home, and of just having lots of fun. Purim is a time of fantasy. Our daughters used to dress up as Queen Esther, making crowns and sewing fancy dresses in which they paraded at synagogue. David dresses up for Purim and at any other time.

Since my children were three, they have known the story of Haman who tried to kill the Jews and lovely Queen Esther who saved them. All children love to sound their gragers, or noisemakers, whenever wicked Haman's name is mentioned during the reading of the Megillah (the Book of Esther). During the reading in our synagogue, the rabbis take part, sometimes dressing up as E.T. or an appropriately popular character.

Purim is a reminder of the Jewish people's deliverance from serious danger in the remote past. Haman, the minister of the Persian king Ahasuerus, wished to exterminate all the Jews of the Persian Empire because he thought the Jew Mordecai had failed to show him proper respect. Mordecai was helped by his cousin and foster daughter, Esther, who became the second queen of King Ahasuerus. Together they foiled wicked Haman's plot. On Adar 13, the day before present-day

Purim, the Jews were to be destroyed. Instead, on this day the Jewish population overcame those who wanted to wipe them out and then celebrated their victory on the following day.

Mordecai and Esther proclaimed that the festival of Purim should be celebrated for all time, by two annual recountings of the story of the Megillah in the synagogue (on the evening prior to and on the day of Purim), a *seudat Purim* or festival meal in the late afternoon of Purim, charity to the poor, and the sending of small baked gifts (*shalach manot*) to friends.

Purim is also a time of getting rid of all the flour and yeast in a Jewish home, since it comes forty days before Passover. In order to use up all the year's flour, many delicacies with risen flour are made.

Despite living in the splendor of the king's palace, Esther never forgot her humble origins. Chick-peas are traditionally eaten at Purim to remind children of the purity of Queen Esther. You can also use them as dried beans inside a decorated paper plate stapled together to make a grager.

A dish my children love to eat at Purim or any time is hummus, which we use as a dip for cut-up vegetables or pieces of pita bread.

HUMMUS

◆ ◆ ◆ ◆ ◆

INGREDIENTS

1 20-ounce can chick-peas
²/₃ cup tahini (sesame paste)
2 cloves garlic
3 lemons
1 teaspoon salt
1 teaspoon cumin
2 tablespoons virgin olive oil
Paprika to taste

EQUIPMENT

Measuring cup
Measuring spoons
Strainer
Food processor
Knife
Mixing bowl
Wooden spoon
Plate

MAKES 2 CUPS

Child with Adult: Drain the chick-peas and put almost all of them in the food processor with the tahini and garlic. Purée.

Child: As you did when making lemonade for the break-the-fast drink at Yom Kippur (see page 50), cut the lemons in half and squeeze them through your fingers. You want ¹/₃ cup of juice. Mix the juice with the chick-pea mixture. Add salt and cumin to taste. Dip your finger in and keep adjusting the taste with the spices until the taste is as you like it.

Child: Spread the mixture out on a plate, dribble a little olive oil on top, and sprinkle with paprika and the remaining chick-peas (you can make a design if you'd like). You can also decorate with cut carrots, olives, parsley—whatever is in your refrigerator.

HAMANTASHEN

◆ ◆ ◆ ◆ ◆ ◆

Haman's hats are the most popular sweet made from flour at Purim. One legend tells us that the three corners of the cookie represent Abraham, Isaac, and Jacob, the founding fathers of Judaism. Although hamantashen traditionally have apricot, poppy-seed, or prune filling, my children like them filled with peanut butter, jelly, and even chocolate chips. Because of those slightly irregular chocolate-chip hamantashen, Purim could become an everyday tradition as far as my children are concerned. We include them on the *shalach manot* plates we take our neighbors.

MAKES ABOUT 36

INGREDIENTS

DOUGH:

⅔ cup (1⅓ sticks) *pareve* margarine or unsalted butter, softened

½ cup sugar

1 egg

3 tablespoons milk or water

½ teaspoon vanilla

2½–3 cups sifted all-purpose unbleached flour

FILLINGS:

Apricot preserves

Peanut butter

Chocolate chips

Nuts

Chopped apples

EQUIPMENT

Measuring cups

Measuring spoons

Mixing bowl

Wooden spoon

Sifter

Knife

Rolling pin

Baking sheets

Pancake turner

Cooling rack

Child: Using a wooden spoon, cream the margarine or butter with the sugar. Add the egg and continue creaming until smooth. Add the milk or water and vanilla. Sift the flour and mix it with the margarine mixture until a ball of dough is formed. Divide the dough in 2 cylinders approximately 3 inches in diameter and refrigerate for a few hours or overnight.

Note: If your children are very young, prepare the dough yourself and just let them make the cookies. You can use a food processor for this.

Adult: Preheat oven to 350°.

Child with Adult, then Alone: Using one cylinder of dough at a time (keep the unused portion refrigerated until needed), cut ⅛-inch slices of dough. Roll them out and place 1 teaspoon of filling in the center of each round. Draw the edges up at 3 points to form a triangle and pinch together carefully. Place the triangles on ungreased baking sheets and bake for 20 minutes, or until golden brown. Cool on rack.

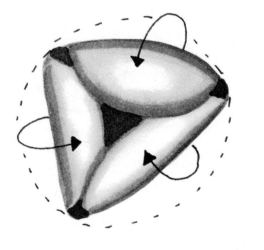

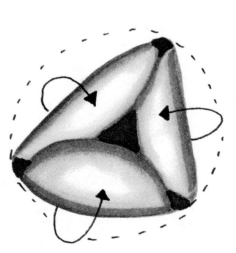

HALVAH

◆ ◆ ◆ ◆ ◆ ◆

Jews from Persia (present-day Iran) are especially proud of Queen Esther's role in the holiday of Purim. A favorite dish of Iranian children is halvah, which they eat after they break the fast of Esther, observed on Adar 13. At nursery school, Merissa learned this recipe for halvah from an Iranian teacher. In between tastes, the children played with Esther and Ahasuerus marionettes they had made with the help of their teacher.

INGREDIENTS

2 cups flour
1½ cups sugar
1 teaspoon ground cinnamon
1 cup vegetable oil
2 cups water
1 cup chopped walnuts

EQUIPMENT

Measuring cups
Measuring spoon
Large frying pan with cover
Wooden spoon
Spatula

MAKES ABOUT 20 SQUARES

Adult with Child: In a frying pan, brown the flour over low heat, watching constantly, for about 20 minutes, stirring occasionally. Remove from heat.

Child: To the flour, add the sugar, cinnamon, and oil. With the pan off the heat, stir for about 5 minutes, keeping the mixture a light brown color.

Adult: Add the water and reheat, stirring for about 5 minutes, until the halvah thickens. Then cover and simmer slowly for 5 minutes more. Fold in the walnuts.

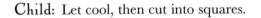

Child: Let cool, then cut into squares.

NO-BAKE MARSHMALLOW COOKIES

◆ ◆ ◆ ◆ ◆

These cookies are a great addition to the *shalach manot* tray. You can make as many as you want.

INGREDIENTS
Marshmallow Fluff
Raisins
Rice Krispies or other cereal
Grated coconut
Chocolate chips
Reese's Pieces or chunky peanut
    butter
Nuts
Vanilla wafers or graham crackers

EQUIPMENT
Plastic wrap
Bowls
Tablespoons
Rolling pin (optional)
Paper candy cups (optional)

Adult: Cut the plastic wrap into 12-inch-long sheets.

Child: Search the kitchen for raisins, cereals, chocolates, or whatever you think will taste good with the Marshmallow Fluff. Place these in individual bowls.

Child: Take about 1 tablespoon of the Marshmallow Fluff and place it in the center of the plastic wrap. Add the ingredients of your choice. Pull all the corners together tightly and squish the package into a ball. Refrigerate for a few minutes.

Child: To make a sandwich cookie, unwrap the marshmallow ball and flatten it between 2 vanilla wafers or 2 graham crackers.

Child: To make a round cookie, put a graham cracker between 2 pieces of plastic wrap and use a rolling pin to roll out the cracker into crumbs. Unwrap the marshmallow ball and roll it in the crumbs. Place it in a paper candy cup for the *shalach manot* tray.

FRUIT YOGHURT POUND CAKE

I always think of this as "a giving cake" because my cousin Dorothy often gives this to me on my birthday and gives it to other people as well as a present many times throughout the year. So why not present this to your neighbors at Purim on your *shalach manot* plates instead of cookies? And, to involve your children, have them choose the kind of yoghurt they want to use in the cake.

INGREDIENTS

2¼ cups all-purpose flour

1½ cups sugar

½ teaspoon salt

½ teaspoon baking soda

Grated rind of 1 lemon

1 teaspoon vanilla

1 cup (2 sticks) soft margarine or
    unsalted butter

1 cup of your favorite yoghurt
    with fruit at the bottom

3 large eggs

GLAZE:

1 cup confectioners' sugar

2 tablespoons lemon juice

EQUIPMENT

Measuring cups

Measuring spoons

10-inch Bundt or tube pan

Large mixing bowl

Electric mixer

MAKES
1 CAKE

Adult: Preheat oven to 325°.

Child: Grease a 10-inch Bundt or tube pan with vegetable spray.

Adult with Child: Measure the flour, sugar, salt, and baking soda and place in a mixing bowl. Using the bowl of an electric mixer combine 1 teaspoon of the lemon rind, vanilla, margarine or butter, yoghurt, and the eggs. Mix well. Fold in the flour ingredients and pour into the greased pan. Bake for 60–70 minutes or until the cake springs back when touched. Cool upright in the pan for 15 minutes. Remove and cool completely.

Child: Combine the confectioners' sugar, the lemon juice, and the remaining rind of the lemon and dribble the mixture over the cake. Serve as is.

PASSOVER

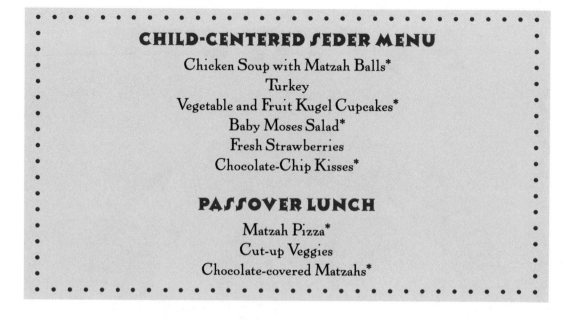

CHILD-CENTERED SEDER MENU

Chicken Soup with Matzah Balls*
Turkey
Vegetable and Fruit Kugel Cupcakes*
Baby Moses Salad*
Fresh Strawberries
Chocolate-Chip Kisses*

PASSOVER LUNCH

Matzah Pizza*
Cut-up Veggies
Chocolate-covered Matzahs*

PASSOVER

The Seder, the festive meal held on the first two nights of Passover, is one of the most delightful events of the year. Seder means "order," but the Seder is really the oldest theatrically produced meal known to mankind. The first Passover feast is described in the Bible, in Exodus, chapter 12. There the Jews ate only roast lamb, bitter herbs, and matzah (unleavened bread) before they fled from Egypt. At the Seder the participants are reminded, both by narration through the reading of the Haggadah and by the foods to be eaten, of the rich heritage of thousands of years and of suffering and deliverance through those millennia.

Pesah means "passing by" or "passing over," and the holiday was called Passover because God passed over the Jewish houses when He slew the firstborn of Egypt. Matzah, unleavened and quickly baked, recalls that the Jews fleeing Egypt had no time to leaven their bread and to bake it properly. Thus we eat no leavened products throughout the eight days of Passover.

Three matzot are placed on the Seder table. One half of one matzah is set aside and served later to mark the ceremonial end of the Seder. It is called the *afikomen,* a Greek word for dessert. Traditionally, the *afikomen* is hidden at the beginning of the Seder and the children search for it at the end of the meal. This is a wonderful way of sustaining their interest throughout the long meal.

Before the Seder, the children help me arrange the symbolic foods on the Seder plate:

Salt water: This represents the bitter tears shed during the years of slavery and the water needed in the spring to make things grow.

Maror: Grated horseradish, bitter herbs, or romaine lettuce are a reminder of the bitterness of slavery.

Zeroa: Roasted shankbone symbolizes the ancient sacrificial lamb of the Passover service and the rebirth of nature in the spring.

Haroset: A mixture of apples, nuts, cinnamon, and wine represents the mortar used by Jewish slaves to build pyramids for the pharaohs.

Karpas: Parsley, or other available greens, recalls the green of the spring and the renewal of faith and hope.

Betzah: A hard-boiled egg, roasted in its shell, represents life and the continuity of existence as well as the special festival offering in the Temple of Jerusalem.

Seder plates and cups are easy for the children to make. Don't forget a cup for the prophet Elijah. Wine cups made of plastic can be decorated with permanent marking pens. Decorated paper plates with cupcake holders glued on are very successful as seder plates. I usually have an adult table and a children's table, so I need two Seder plates. During the service itself, the children sit with us.

We make getting ready for Passover a family spring-cleaning affair. The children help clean their rooms, especially their closets. The kitchen is left for last, with all the *hametz,* or leavened products, brought to the garage. (Some families symbolically sell their *hametz* to neighbors and buy it back at the end of Passover. From Purim to Passover we try to use up all our flour, rice, and cereals, so there is not much to get rid of.) Traditional families even change their dishes. The day before Passover, we take a feather or the lulav saved from Sukkot and look for *hametz* around the house. I always plant some pieces of bread for the children to find.

On the day of the Seder—one of the busiest of the year for me—the children keep occupied by coloring and decorating. They contribute by making name tags, setting the table, putting a pillow in Daddy's chair, and helping to make the haroset, the last dish to be prepared for the Seder.

We try to make our Seder as participatory as possible. It is very important to go through all the steps: dipping the finger in wine, making everyone taste the bitter herbs and parsley, and singing the songs. Children can relate to these actions, and they are very visual learning mechanisms.

At our Seder, the children always perform a Passover play. As on Friday night, while the adults linger over their main course, the children leave the room and put together a skit of the exodus of the Jews from Egypt.

Children can make their own haggadahs at school or at home and then have them on the table. We have saved those from our children for years, and I put them out at the Seder. Another possibility for organizing a Seder with children is to ask each child to write a poem or story or to draw a picture about some part of the Passover story weeks ahead of time. The host then photocopies the contributions and puts together a haggadah for that year.

There is a great deal of packaged and prepared Passover food on the market. Stay away from them—things you make yourself are much better and more fun.

HAROSET

INGREDIENTS

8 apples
⅔ cup almonds
3 tablespoons sugar, or to taste
½ teaspoon ground cinnamon
Grated rind of 1 lemon
4 tablespoons sweet red wine

EQUIPMENT

Measuring cup
Measuring spoons
Vegetable peeler
Knife
Wooden chopping bowl
Old-fashioned chopper or food
  processor

MAKES ABOUT 3 CUPS

Child: Peel the apples and cut them in quarters, removing the core. Using your chopping bowl and chopper, chop together all the ingredients. The apples and almonds should be about the size of the chunks in chunky peanut butter. Add red wine to taste.

BABY MOSES SALAD

I find the Seder preparation such a strenuous task that the more I can allow my children to create, the better it is for me. They design this dish for each person (we have about thirty guests) and have fun doing it. Depending on the age of your children, you can have the ingredients cut up ahead of time and just let them do the assembling.

INGREDIENTS
Carrots
Raisins or black olives
Green peppers
Parboiled asparagus
Romaine lettuce leaves
Radishes
Vinaigrette dressing

EQUIPMENT
Vegetable peeler
Paring knife

MAKE A SALAD FOR EACH PERSON

Adult with Child: Peel the carrots and slice them into rounds. Cut the olives in half, if you will need them for your decoration. Cut the green peppers and asparagus into strips as long as you need.

Child: Place a romaine leaf on each salad plate to be the cradle or little ark. Decorate it as you would imagine a baby Moses in his cradle, with his face, arms, and so on.

Child with Adult: If you wish, add radish flowers for decoration. These are made by carefully cutting off the top of a radish and then slicing down the sides, about one-third of the way down, in 4 or 5 places.

Child: Remember that adults like dressing, which you can dribble on top of the salad. They also tend to like asparagus better than you do.

VEGETABLE AND FRUIT KUGEL CUPCAKES

A kugel, usually a bread pudding cooked with the Sabbath cholent, was the kind of slightly sweet East European dish we think of as dessert. Sugary desserts were actually a very late invention. This kugel, made in the form of cupcakes, can be eaten as a vegetable side dish or a dessert.

MAKES
24

INGREDIENTS

2 apples

1 large sweet potato

4 carrots

1 cup matzah meal

½ cup (1 stick) *pareve* margarine, melted

1 teaspoon salt

1 teaspoon baking soda*

1 teaspoon ground cinnamon

1 teaspoon ground nutmeg

EQUIPMENT

Measuring cups

Measuring spoon

Vegetable peeler

Grater or food processor

Mixing bowl

Wooden spoon

24 paper muffin cups

Muffin tins for 24 cupcakes

Rubber scraper

Adult: Preheat oven to 350°.

* Baking soda is kosher for Passover because, when added to matzah meal, it will not leaven it any further.

Child Alone, or with Adult: Peel and grate the apples, sweet potato, and carrots. Mix with the rest of the ingredients. Place the paper muffin cups in the muffin tins. Pour the batter into the cups. They should be two-thirds full. Bake for 20–25 minutes, or until done.

MATZAH PIZZA

My kids love pizza and this is an easy substitute for lunch or dinner during Passover.

INGREDIENTS
1 full sheet of matzah
½ cup prepared kosher-for-
    Passover tomato sauce
½ cup grated kosher-for-Passover
    cheese

EQUIPMENT
Baking sheet
Measuring cups
Spoon

SERVES
1

Adult: Preheat oven to 400°.

Child: Place the matzah on the baking sheet. Spread the tomato sauce on top, covering as much as you can. Sprinkle the cheese over the sauce.

Adult with Child: Bake the matzah pizza for about 5 minutes or until the top is melted and bubbly. Remove from the oven to a plate and enjoy eating with a knife and fork or just your hands.

CHOCOLATE-CHIP KISSES

INGREDIENTS

1 cup roughly chopped walnuts,
   pecans, and chocolate chips
3 large eggs
1 cup sugar
½ teaspoon vanilla (optional)

EQUIPMENT

Measuring cups
Measuring spoon
Large mixing bowl
2 smaller mixing bowls
Electric mixer or wire whisk
Large spoon
Parchment paper
Baking sheets
Pancake turner

MAKES
ABOUT
36

Adult: Preheat oven to 300°.

Child: Break up the nuts into pieces at least as small as the chocolate chips. Separate the eggs—one at a time, in case they break. Here's the Greek-Jewish way: Make a tiny hole in the end of the egg. Holding the egg in the middle, let the white run out into a bowl. Save the yolks for another use.

Adult with Child: Beat the egg whites until they form peaks. Gradually beat in the sugar and vanilla until the whites are stiff.

Child: Gently stir the nuts and chocolate chips into the egg whites with a spoon. Drop the batter on parchment paper on a baking sheet in tear-drops. Bake for 20–30 minutes, until the kisses are hard but still white.

Note: For children who don't like nuts, simply substitute more choco-late chips.

PAſſOVER-ſTYLE FARFEL AND CHEEſE

It seems to me that every Passover food article stresses food for the Seder itself. What about those in-between meals when you cannot let the children have their usual macaroni and cheese, pizza, or hamburgers on buns? Merissa's teacher taught us this recipe.

INGREDIENTſ

3 large eggs

3 cups matzah farfel

Vegetable spray

½ pound kosher-for-Passover cheddar cheese

1½ cups sour cream

6 tablespoons (¾ stick) unsalted butter or margarine

2 cups milk

1 teaspoon salt

¼ teaspoon pepper

EQUIPMENT

Measuring cups

Measuring spoons

Old-fashioned egg beater or wire whisk

Mixing bowl

Knife

Spoon

2-quart baking dish with cover

Pancake turner

ſERVEſ
8

Adult with Child: This is a great way to talk about the old days when you were young and used an egg beater! Break 2 of the eggs and beat well with the egg beater or whisk.

Child: Pour the beaten eggs over the farfel and mix well. Pour into the baking dish greased with vegetable spray.

Adult: Preheat oven to 350°.

Child: Being careful with the knife, dice the cheddar cheese into small bits. Add the cheese to the farfel. Using a spoon, add the sour cream in dollops and dot with butter or margarine. Mix together the milk, remaining egg, salt, and pepper, and pour it over the casserole. (A child can be very creative in this preparation because basically it doesn't matter in the final product.)

Child with Adult: Cover and bake for 30 minutes. Uncover and let brown for 10–15 minutes more. Scoop out onto plates.

MATZAH BREI

What would Passover be without matzah brei for breakfast? David is now old enough to make this alone. Before, we worked together on this variation of a classic theme.

SERVES
4–6

INGREDIENTS

3 matzot
2 large eggs
Salt to taste
1 tablespoon honey
½ teaspoon ground cinnamon
2 tablespoons (¼ stick) margarine
   for frying

EQUIPMENT

Measuring spoons
Mixing bowl
Paper towels
Fork or wire whisk
Spoon
Frying pan
Metal spatula

Child: Break up the matzot and put in lukewarm water for a few minutes. Drain on paper towels and squeeze dry. Beat the eggs. Mix them well with the salt, honey, cinnamon, and the matzah.

Adult: Heat the margarine in the frying pan. Fry 2 tablespoons of batter at a time, patting the center down a bit. Turn over and fry until golden. Eat as is, or with additional honey.

CHOCOLATE-COVERED MATZAHS

INGREDIENTS

6 ounces bittersweet chocolate, kosher for Passover

2 tablespoons water

1 sheet of matzah, cut into 6 rectangles

EQUIPMENT

Double boiler

Tongs (optional)

Wax paper

Baking sheet

MAKES
6

Adult: Melt the chocolate with water over warm water in the double boiler.

Child: Using tongs or your fingers, dip the matzah in the hot melted chocolate. Place it on wax paper on a baking sheet. Let it harden for a few minutes in the refrigerator.

Child: Lick the pot as the first, very necessary step in cleaning up!

ISRAEL INDEPENDENCE DAY MENU

Kibbutz Vegetable Salad*

Hummus*

Vegetarian Chopped Liver*

Israeli Falafel*

Jaffa Orange Sorbet*

Golda Meir's Chocolate-Chip Cookies*

ISRAEL INDEPENDENCE DAY BRUNCH

Shakshouka*

Kubbanah*

Israeli Coin Carrot Salad*

Cucumber-Yoghurt Salad*

Apricot Fruit Leathers*

IRAEL INDEPENDENCE DAY

Merissa used to think that Israel was a person because at her nursery school a cake with candles was served for its "birthday." Israel Independence Day, celebrated each year in mid-May, is the anniversary of the creation in 1948 of the new State of Israel. In Israel it is a national holiday, with picnicking and parades. Plastic hammers, which make a squeaking sound when hit on someone's head, are used in the streets as revelers march along. I remember how surprised I was to see Teddy Kollek, the then mayor of Jerusalem, being bopped on the head like any other person as he joined the revelers on one Independence Day.

In this country, Jewish schools have birthday cakes, and many Jewish community centers and synagogues have celebrations. Make your own falafel party with the help of your children this year.

KIBBUTZ VEGETABLE SALAD

On an Israeli kibbutz (collective farm), salads are very often do-it-yourself affairs. *Kibbutzniks* have the custom of putting the raw ingredients on the table and making individual salads.

For breakfast on a kibbutz, often eaten at 4:00 A.M. so that the work can be done before the heat of day, workers eat at long tables. A large bowl is filled with whole green peppers, cucumbers, tomatoes, scallions, and sometimes kohlrabi. There are smaller bowls of olives, hard-boiled eggs, cheeses, and bread. Salad dressing is made with the lemons that grow in the Land of Israel. The food is cut up in little pieces and makeshift salads prepared to the taste of the diner. The following recipe is a great exercise for children in learning to use a knife. Give them a plastic knife for starters. Four or five years old is as early an age as you want to begin this.

INGREDIENTS

1 tomato

1 cucumber

2 scallions

2 tablespoons chopped fresh
    parsley

1 green pepper

1 lemon, at room temperature

6 tablespoons vegetable oil or olive
    oil, or a combination of the two

1 clove garlic, mashed

Salt and freshly ground pepper to
    taste

EQUIPMENT

Measuring spoons

Plastic knife

Cutting board

Knife

Fork

Small bowl

**SERVES
4**

Adult with Child: Show the children how to hold a vegetable firmly with one hand and then gently but firmly cut a slice into the vegetable. Let them take turns until all the vegetables are diced (do not peel the tomato). Mix all the vegetables together.

Child: Cut the lemon in half. Make sure it is at room temperature. Take a fork and pierce the pulp of each side of the lemon. Then, using one hand like a strainer, with the other hand squeeze the lemon through your fingers, catching the seeds before they get mixed with the juice.

Child: Carefully dribble the lemon juice and then the oil over the vegetables. Add the garlic (unless you find garlic yucky) and season with salt and pepper as you like.

Note: You can also add black olives, carrots, kohlrabi, lettuce, etc. Another way of serving this salad is just to place the freshly picked vegetables on the table and let people make their own salad, cutting up and seasoning as they go along.

I/RAELI FALAFEL

Probably more than any other food eaten in Israel, falafel (chick-pea patties), the primary street food, has gained international status. It is eaten
from street carts from Tel Aviv to Paris to Los Angeles to Cairo. Have a
falafel party with your family, stuffing the falafel into pita bread with sliced
lettuce, sour pickles or turnips, and hot sauce.

INGREDIENT/

2 cups chick-peas which have been
   soaked in water overnight

1 large onion, chopped

2 tablespoons finely chopped
   parsley

1 large egg

1 teaspoon salt

1 teaspoon dried hot red pepper
   flakes

2 cloves garlic

1 teaspoon cumin

Dash of coriander

1/2 cup fine bulgur wheat which
   has been soaked in water for
   1 hour

Vegetable oil for deep-frying

EQUIPMENT

Measuring cups

Measuring spoons

Mixing bowl

Blender or food processor

Falafel maker (optional)

Deep fryer or heavy pot

Slotted spoon

Paper towels

MAKE/
ABOUT
24

Child with Adult: Mix the chick-peas with the onion. Add the parsley,
egg, and spices. Whirl in a blender or food processor. Add the bulgur

wheat and continue to whirl until the mixture forms a small ball. Refrigerate for at least 1 hour. Form the chick-pea mixture into small balls about the size of a walnut, or use a falafel maker if you can find one.

Adult with Child: Flatten the patties slightly before deep-frying them in oil until golden brown on each side. Drain the falafel on paper towels.

GOLDA MEIR'S
CHOCOLATE-CHIP COOKIES

Golda Meir was an American woman from Milwaukee, Wisconsin, who decided to live on a kibbutz in Israel. She became the prime minister of the country and a heroine to women around the world. Even while she led her country, she entertained friends and visitors in her simple kitchen. One of her favorite foods, linking America and Israel, was chocolate-chip cookies, which she varied by adding Jaffa orange juice to the classic recipe she had learned in her youth in Wisconsin.

MAKES ABOUT 40

INGREDIENTS

1 cup (2 sticks) unsalted butter or *pareve* margarine
½ cup white sugar
½ cup firmly packed light-brown sugar
1¾ cups all-purpose flour
1 teaspoon baking soda
1 teaspoon salt
2 eggs
2 teaspoons orange juice
12 ounces chocolate chips

EQUIPMENT

Measuring cups
Measuring spoons
Mixing bowls
Wooden spoon
Sifter
Electric mixer or food processor
Greased baking sheets
Tablespoon
Pancake turner
Cooling rack

Adult: Preheat oven to 350°.

Child: Using a wooden spoon, cream together the butter and the white and brown sugar. In a large bowl, sift together the flour, baking soda, and salt. Mix together the butter and sugar mixture, the flour mixture, and the eggs and orange juice. With a wooden spoon, beat until everything is smooth and well combined, or use an electric mixer or food processor until well blended. (If you beat by hand, take turns at it—it's fun.) Stir in the chocolate chips.

Child: Drop the dough by tablespoons onto the baking sheets about 3 inches apart.

Adult: Bake for 10–12 minutes, or until golden. Remove from the oven, let sit a few minutes, and transfer with a pancake turner to a rack to cool.

JAFFA ORANGE SORBET

To be really authentic, this dessert should be made with oranges from Jaffa, Israel.

INGREDIENTS
¼ cup sugar
1 cup water
1 cup orange juice
4 oranges

EQUIPMENT
Measuring cups
Saucepan
Ice trays
Rubber scraper
Knife
Grapefruit knife
Spoon
Bowl
Egg beater or whisk

SERVES
4

Child: In a saucepan, dissolve the sugar in the water.

Adult: Bring to a boil, uncovered, and boil for 5 minutes.

Child: Pour the orange juice into the sugar syrup. Pour the mixture into an ice tray and put it in the freezer.

Adult: Cut the tops off the oranges.

Child with Adult: Using a grapefruit knife, cut out the inside of the oranges. Eat the fruit.

Child: When the mixture starts to freeze around the edges, remove it from the freezer and put it into a bowl. Using an egg beater or whisk, beat it well. Spoon it into the cored-out oranges and put them in the freezer until the mixture hardens like sherbet.

SHAKSHOUKA (EGGS IN TOMATO SAUCE)

Shakshouka is one of those onomatopoeic words in Hebrew—a word that sounds like what it is. It means, literally, mixed-up, which is what you do in this Moroccan recipe for scrambled eggs turned Israeli. Making eggs is an American Sunday morning family ritual that is a pleasure to share with your children. This recipe is a great way to learn how to make scrambled eggs. You know your family best, so let the kids add their favorite vegetables and cheese, from cheddar to feta. When I lived in Israel I used to make this with or without the tomatoes, sometimes adding cream cheese without the tomatoes as an evening meal.

INGREDIENTS

2 scallions, chopped small
1 small green pepper, diced
2 tablespoons vegetable oil
2 medium tomatoes
4 large eggs
Low-fat cream cheese or feta
Salt and pepper to taste

EQUIPMENT

Sharp knife
Large frying pan with lid
Grater
Mixing bowl
Spoon
Egg beater

SERVES 4

Adult with Child: Cut up the scallions and green pepper.

Adult: In a large frying pan with a lid, quickly sauté the scallions and green pepper (and any other vegetables you choose) in vegetable oil until the vegetables are soft.

Adult with Child: Cut up the tomatoes into a bowl.

Adult with Child: Add the tomato liquid and pulp to the vegetables, cover and cook over a low heat for 20 minutes.

Adult with Child: Beat the eggs well and pour over the vegetables in the pan. Add dollops of cream cheese or crumbled feta cheese. Using a fork, gently scramble the eggs well. Then cover and cook for about 3–4 minutes until the eggs are set. Sprinkle with salt and pepper and serve with a spoon. Do not overcook.

Note: Among the many possible variations, you can add a minced clove of garlic or 3–4 slices of red pepper to the vegetables as they sauté.

SHAVUOT BRUNCH

Bagels*
Homemade Butter*
Apple and Cream Cheese Spread*
Easy Cheese Blintzes* or French Toast*
Fruitful Salad*
Zucchini Bread*

SHAVUOT LUNCH

Kids' Quiche with Veggies*
Homemade Peanut Butter* Sandwiches
Green Salad
Shavuot Milk Shake*
Fruit Yoghurt Pound Cake*

SHAVUOT

Shavuot marks the day when Moses received the Torah on Mount Sinai. It is also a nature holiday celebrating the time when farmers brought the first fruits of their harvest to the holy Temple in Jerusalem. It falls at the time of year when cream and milk are traditionally the richest.

HOMEMADE BUTTER

Shavuot is the perfect holiday to show children how to make their own butter. With the symbolism of the white Torah on Mount Sinai, and coming at the time of year when there is so much grass that cows eat more and thus produce more milk, it is traditionally a milk holiday.

INGREDIENTS

½ cup heavy cream per child

MAKES ABOUT ¼ CUP OR ½ STICK

EQUIPMENT

Jar with a secure cap

Child: Pour the cream into the jar. Tighten the cap and shake until the cream separates into butter and whey or liquid. Pour off the whey.

BAGELS

There is no recipe more traditionally Jewish or more fun for children to make than bagels. In Judaism, bagels have a role in many life-cycle events. Being round, they symbolize the endless circle of life. They are served at circumcisions and naming ceremonies.

This recipe comes from Mark Talisman, who has been baking ever since he was seven years old. When his daughter, Jessica, was a toddler, he tried to figure out a productive, creative, and tactile activity for her from 5:00 A.M., when she woke up, until 7:00. Bagel making was the answer. Dough is more fun than clay; she could eat the bagels; and, when her younger brother Rafi came along, he could teethe on the lopsided figure eights she and her father made for him.

When you are making these with children, please don't be a perfectionist. Any roundish shape will do.

MAKES
20–24

INGREDIENTS

2 tablespoons (¼ stick) butter or
  margarine
1 cup milk, scalded
2 tablespoons (2 packages) dry
  yeast
Pinch of sugar
1 cup warm water
8 cups (about) unbleached all-
  purpose flour
1 tablespoon salt
3 quarts water
4 tablespoons honey
Sesame or poppy seeds

EQUIPMENT

Measuring spoons
Measuring cups
Saucepan
Bowl
Spoon
Greased mixing bowl
Clean dish towel
Large pot with lid
Slotted spoon
Greased baking sheet

melt butter in milk

mix sugar, yeast & water

blend in flour & salt

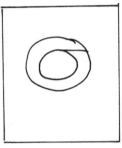

knead dough well

cover & let rise

roll piece of dough

into a snakelike shape

twist into a circle

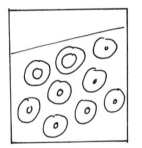

place on floured surface

boil water & honey

drop in bagels

place on baking sheet

bake for 30 minutes

eat!

Adult with Child: Melt the butter or margarine in the scalded milk. Mix the yeast with a pinch of sugar in the warm water and make sure it bubbles. Mix together the milk and yeast mixtures. Gradually blend in the flour and the salt until a soft, sticky dough is formed. Knead well and place in a greased bowl. Cover with a clean towel and let rise in a warm place about 1 hour, until the dough has grown to almost double its size.

Note: To shorten waiting time for impatient children, do the first step yourself. Let the dough rise, and refrigerate it until you are ready to use it.

Child: Knead the dough again on a floured surface. Break off a piece about the size of a plum and roll it into a 5½-inch-long snakelike shape, tapering the dough at the ends. Twist it into a circle and press the ends together. Place on a floured surface. Continue until all the dough is used up. Let stand, uncovered, until the dough begins to rise (about 10 minutes).

Adult: Preheat oven to 400°. Boil about 3 quarts water with the honey.

Adult First, Then Child: Drop the bagels one by one into the boiling honey water, boiling a few at a time. Cover and wait until the water boils again. With a slotted spoon, turn the bagels over, cover again, and wait until the water boils (about 2 minutes). Remove to a greased baking sheet.

Child: Sprinkle the bagels with sesame or poppy seeds and bake about 30 minutes, or until golden. These bagels freeze well.

APPLE AND CREAM CHEESE SPREAD

INGREDIENTS
1 small apple
½ teaspoon ground cinnamon
1 teaspoon sugar
4 ounces cream cheese

EQUIPMENT
Measuring spoons
Vegetable peeler
Apple corer
Food processor

MAKES
½ CUP

Child: Carefully peel the apple and remove the core.

Adult with Child: Using the steel blade of the food processor, whirl together the apple and all the remaining ingredients. Spread on a bagel.

CUCUMBER-YOGHURT SALAD

Yoghurt is probably the oldest milk dish in the world. Once upon a time, a man was riding a camel and put some goat or sheep milk in his pouch. After he went through the desert and tasted the milk, it had changed into yoghurt. In Israel, children eat yoghurt the way we drink milk in the United States.

INGREDIENTS

2 small cucumbers

1 apple

2 hard-boiled eggs

2 cups yoghurt

1 cup cold water

3 ice cubes

¼ cup white or dark raisins

¼ cup chopped walnuts

3 tablespoons fresh mint

Salt to taste

EQUIPMENT

Measuring cups

Measuring spoon

Vegetable peeler

Knife

Glass or ceramic bowl

Wooden spoon

SERVES 4–6

Child: Peel the cucumbers, apple, and eggs. Dice them. Then mix together all the ingredients very well. Cover and let sit in the refrigerator for a few hours or overnight.

EASY CHEESE BLINTZES

Cheese is the most traditional food at Shavuot. These blintzes are great fun for children to make. Using a toaster oven, they can be made in school.

SERVES 6

INGREDIENTS

6 slices white bread

8 tablespoons cream cheese

1 teaspoon ground cinnamon

8 tablespoons (1 stick) butter

EQUIPMENT

Measuring spoons

Rolling pin

Sharp knife

Baking pan to fit toaster oven

Toaster oven

Adult: Preheat toaster oven to 350° (of course, you can use a regular oven as well).

Child: Roll out the bread with a rolling pin, as thin as possible.

Adult with Child: Using a sharp knife, cut the bread into circles.

Child: Smear the bread circles with cream cheese and a bit of cinnamon. Roll them up like jelly rolls.

Adult: Melt the butter in the baking pan.

Child: Roll the blintzes in the butter, put them in the baking pan, and bake for 10 minutes.

FRENCH TOAST

INGREDIENTS
3 eggs
½ teaspoon vanilla
1 teaspoon grated orange rind
½ teaspoon ground cinnamon
¼ cup milk
6 slices hallah ¾ inch thick
Butter or margarine and oil for
  frying

EQUIPMENT
Measuring spoons
Measuring cup
Mixing bowl
Fork or wire whisk
9 by 13-inch pan
Griddle or frying pan
Pancake turner

SERVES
6

Child: Beat the eggs well. Add the vanilla, orange rind, cinnamon, and milk. Pour into a 9 by 13-inch pan. Add the hallah slices and let sit for about 15 minutes. Turn and let sit for a few minutes more.

Adult: Heat a griddle or frying pan with butter or margarine and oil, about 1 tablespoon altogether for each slice of hallah. Fry the egg-drenched hallah on both sides and serve with maple syrup.

Child: When you have mastered this, try making breakfast for your Mom or Dad one day.

SHAVUOT MILK SHAKE

In my experience children prefer smooth to crunchy except when it comes to ice cream or icy drinks. This is a great milk drink for Shavuot or for a snack at any time of the year.

MAKES
1 SHAKE

INGREDIENTS

1 cup milk or frozen yoghurt
½ cup sliced strawberries,
    bananas, or raspberries
2 ice cubes
Sugar or honey (optional)

EQUIPMENT

Blender or food processor
Measuring cups
Glass

Child: Measure the milk or frozen yoghurt and the fruit and place in the blender or food processor. Add 2 ice cubes.

Child with Adult: Process until crunchy smooth. Add a teaspoon or so of sugar or honey if too tart. If using frozen yoghurt, you may need to add some milk if it is too thick.

Note: Try your own creative combinations of frozen yoghurt or milk and fruit.

APRICOT FRUIT LEATHERS

We think that fruit leathers were invented in America. Wrong! Even in biblical times before sugar, children had a sweet tooth. They snacked on fruit leathers and date jam before anyone knew what a cookie sweetened with sugar and puffed up with baking powder was. Who knows, maybe this is the oldest snack food known to mankind!

MAKES ABOUT 4

INGREDIENTS
1 cup dried apricots
Hot water to cover

EQUIPMENT
Measuring cup
Mixing bowl
Strainer
Mortar and pestle or food
　　processor
Plastic wrap or wax paper
Rolling pin

Child: Place the apricots in water to cover and let soften. This will take about 15 minutes.

Adult with Child: Drain the apricots in a strainer and put them in a mortar and pestle or food processor. The mortar and pestle is great fun for the children to use to mash up the apricots. Once the fruit has been pulverized, place the leathers between 2 pieces of wax paper or plastic wrap. Roll out as thin as possible and leave to dry for about 2 days in the wrap. Remove wrap, roll up the leathers, and, using scissors, cut into 3-inch widths. Nosh for a snack.

APPLE PANCAKES

Shavuot is a fine time to serve these apple pancakes with a dollop of sour cream on top. Try them for brunch at Shavuot or throughout the year, and watch them puff up!

INGREDIENTS

½ cup all-purpose flour
½ teaspoon salt
Dash of ground nutmeg
2 large eggs
½ cup regular or skim milk
4 tablespoons (½ stick) unsalted
   butter or margarine
1 apple, cored, peeled, and sliced
   paper thin
Juice of ½ lemon
Confectioners' sugar for sprinkling

EQUIPMENT

Mixing bowl
Measuring cup
Measuring spoons
Spoon
12-inch heavy frying pan with
   ovenproof handle
Apple corer
Sharp knife
Spatula

SERVES
4

Child with Adult: Using a mixing bowl, carefully measure the dry ingredients. Add the eggs and the milk and stir to mix but do not beat.

Adult: Place the butter in the frying pan and melt it over a medium heat. Preheat oven to 425°.

Child with Adult: Swirl the butter around the frying pan and then add the batter and spread evenly. Arrange the apple slices on top of the batter, sprinkle with the lemon juice, and place in the oven to bake for 12–15 minutes, or until puffy and crisp around the edges. Keep checking the oven. This is easy if your oven has a window—and it is fun to watch the pancake puff up.

Adult: Remove the pancake from the oven. Using a spatula, carefully lift it up and put it on a plate.

Child: Sprinkle the top with confectioners' sugar and serve.

Note: You can also substitute chocolate chips for the apples. Umm good!

INDEX